Legal Notice

Title: Candlestick Mastery Beginner to Pro in 66 Patterns: Learn Technical
Analysis with Charts and Challenges
Author: The Million-Dollar Margin Club MMCVisions
Printed Version ISBN: 979-8-9890300-8-8
Publisher: MMCVisions Publishing
Publication Date: February 2024
For permission requests, contact: MMCVisions@gmail.com
Website: million-dollar-marginclub.com
YouTube Channel Million-Dollar-Margin Club

The Million-Dollar Margin Club™

MMCVisions Publishing

Other Books by MMCVisions Publishing
Available on Amazon

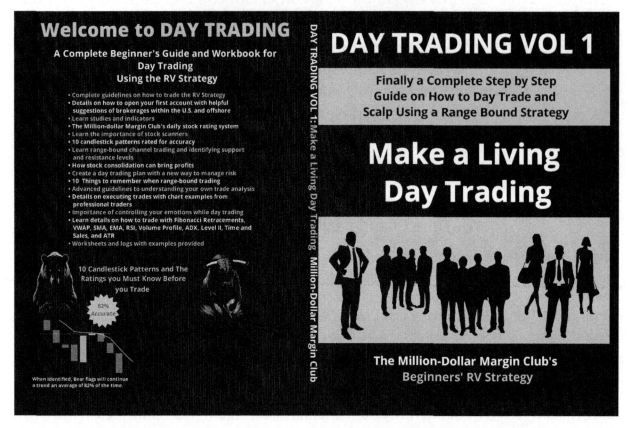

Welcome to DAY TRADING

A Complete Beginner's Guide and Workbook for
Day Trading
Using the RV Strategy

- Complete guidelines on how to trade the RV Strategy
- Details on how to open your first account with helpful
  suggestions of brokerages within the U.S. and offshore
- Learn studies and indicators
- The Million-dollar Margin Club's daily stock rating system
- Learn the importance of stock scanners
- 10 candlestick patterns rated for accuracy
- Learn range-bound channel trading and identifying support
  and resistance levels
- How stock consolidation can bring profits
- Create a day trading plan with a new way to manage risk
- 10 Things to remember when range-bound trading
- Advanced guidelines to understanding your own trade analysis
- Details on executing trades with chart examples from
  professional traders
- Importance of controlling your emotions while day trading
- Learn details on how to trade with Fibonacci Retracements,
  VWAP, SMA, EMA, RSI, Volume Profile, ADX, Level II, Time and
  Sales, and ATR
- Worksheets and logs with examples provided

10 Candlestick Patterns and The
Ratings you Must Know Before
you Trade

82% Accurate

When identified, Bear flags will continue
a trend an average of 82% of the time.

DAY TRADING VOL 1: Make a Living Day Trading Million-Dollar Margin Club

DAY TRADING VOL 1

Finally a Complete Step by Step
Guide on How to Day Trade and
Scalp Using a Range Bound Strategy

Make a Living
Day Trading

The Million-Dollar Margin Club's
Beginners' RV Strategy

Million-Dollar Margin Club's best selling book: **DAY TRADING VOL 1**

The Million-Dollar Margin Club's 3 best known strategies to become a successful trader are:

The RV range-bound (channel trading) strategy, also identified by **AI** as one of the top 5 strategies currently traded, follows these basic steps.
The Million-Dollar Margin Club developed professional **rating systems** used to find the stocks they will trade each day. These systems are detailed in the book DAY TRADING VOL 1.
Trade large cap stocks in a consolidating pattern.
Create a channel to trade in using the ATR levels over a 14 day period.
Use Fibonacci Retracement Levels and other pivot points to identify support and resistance levels that create channels to trade within ATR levels.
Use basic scalping indicators to gauge volume and momentum within the channels' identified ceilings and floors.

The Open Strategy: *New book coming soon.* Do not enter the trade until the price action *breaks the premarket high or low levels.* Then use common support and resistance levels to determine reversal.

The Escalator Strategy: Once the price action *breaks the ATR levels* determined in the RV Strategy, wait for a retest of the ATR level, then enter a position and follow common support and resistance levels to manage your trade.

Other Books by MMCVisions Publishing
Available on Amazon

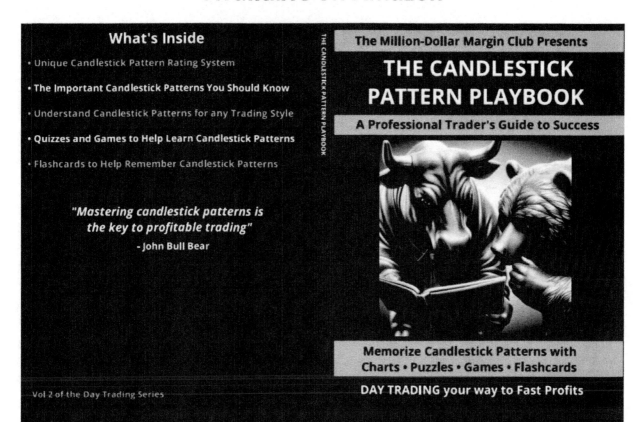

What's Inside

- Unique Candlestick Pattern Rating System

- **The Important Candlestick Patterns You Should Know**

- Understand Candlestick Patterns for any Trading Style

- **Quizzes and Games to Help Learn Candlestick Patterns**

- Flashcards to Help Remember Candlestick Patterns

*"Mastering candlestick patterns is
the key to profitable trading"*
- John Bull Bear

THE CANDLESTICK PATTERN PLAYBOOK

Vol 2 of the Day Trading Series

The Million-Dollar Margin Club Presents

THE CANDLESTICK PATTERN PLAYBOOK

A Professional Trader's Guide to Success

**Memorize Candlestick Patterns with
Charts • Puzzles • Games • Flashcards**

DAY TRADING your way to Fast Profits

TABLE OF CONTENTS

Have fun as You Learn Your Candlestick Patterns with These Helpful Flashcards

Other Books by MMCVisions Publishing
Available on Amazon

COMPANION BOOK TO DAY TRADING VOL 1

Additional Tools and Worksheets for Day Trading Using a Range Bound Strategy

Stock Rating System and Log Sheets for the RV Strategy

Million-Dollar Margin Club's Beginner Strategy

TRADING
JOURNAL
LOG BOOK

A Complete Trading Tool with
Logs • Watchlists • Criteria for Trade Selection
Rules for Trading • Steps for Analysis
Weekly Performance Logs • Trading Plans
Contacts • Notes • Glossary of Terms

Stocks • Forex • Options • Crypto • Futures

OPTIONS TRADING LOGBOOK AND JOURNAL

TRADE LIKE A PROFESSIONAL

THE MILLION-DOLLAR MARGIN CLUB SHARES 4 TRADERS' PROFITABLE STRATEGIES USED IN WORLDWIDE COMPETITION

FUTURES TRADING LOGBOOK AND JOURNAL

TRADE LIKE A PROFESSIONAL

THE MILLION-DOLLAR MARGIN CLUB SHARES 4 TRADERS' PROFITABLE STRATEGIES USED IN WORLDWIDE COMPETITION

Other Books by MMCVisions Publishing
Available on Amazon

CRYPTO TRADING LOGBOOK AND JOURNAL

TRADE LIKE A PROFESSIONAL

THE MILLION-DOLLAR MARGIN CLUB SHARES 4 TRADERS' PROFITABLE STRATEGIES USED IN WORLDWIDE COMPETITION

STOCK TRADING LOGBOOK AND JOURNAL

TRADE LIKE A PROFESSIONAL

THE MILLION-DOLLAR MARGIN CLUB SHARES 4 TRADERS' PROFITABLE STRATEGIES USED IN WORLDWIDE COMPETITION

PENNY STOCK TRADING LOGBOOK AND JOURNAL

TRADE LIKE A PROFESSIONAL

THE MILLION-DOLLAR MARGIN CLUB SHARES 4 TRADERS' PROFITABLE STRATEGIES USED IN WORLDWIDE COMPETITION

FOREX TRADING LOGBOOK AND JOURNAL

TRADE LIKE A PROFESSIONAL

THE MILLION-DOLLAR MARGIN CLUB SHARES 4 TRADERS' PROFITABLE STRATEGIES USED IN WORLDWIDE COMPETITION

Follow the "Million-Dollar Margin Club MMCVisions" to get new release updates on their Amazon Author's Page

https://amzn.to/3UOplQJ

Million-Dollar-Margin Club YouTube channel:
bit.ly/3tNzDFA

TABLE OF CONTENTS

Chapter 1

The Origin of the Candlestick

The Importance of Candlestick Patterns

Candlestick Patterns Used with

Different Trading Styles

A Basic Candlestick

Candlestick Patterns

The Origin of the Candlestick

To understand the origin of candlestick patterns, we must embark on a journey back in time to ancient Japan. During the 17th century a legendary rice trader named Munehisa Homma, developed a revolutionary method of analyzing price action. Homma observed that emotions and market psychology played a crucial role in determining price movements, a concept far ahead of its time.

Homma's revolutionary insights led to the development of the first primitive form of candlestick charting, which employed a series of vertical lines resembling candlesticks. These candlesticks depicted the open, high, low, and close prices for a specific time period. This groundbreaking visual representation of price action gained popularity and laid the foundation for what would later become known as candlestick patterns.

Originally in trading, there were 9 identified candlestick "Patterns" including: Marubozu, Doji, Hammer, Shooting Star, Spinning Top, Hanging Man, Engulfing Pattern, Dark Cloud Cover, and Piercing Pattern. The first 6 of these are single candlesticks and the last 3 are multiple candlestick patterns.

The 20th century witnessed the gradual adoption of candlestick patterns by western traders and investors. Notably, in the 1930's, a financial journalist named Charles Dow incorporated the principles of candlestick analysis into his Dow Theory, which laid the foundation for modern technical analysis. This integration helped bridge the gap between eastern and western trading methodologies, leading to further refinement and wider acceptance of candlestick patterns.

Now, with the advent of computer technology, pattern recognition in candlestick charts has become more accurate and efficient by using algorithms to identify patterns automatically and quickly. Candlestick patterns can readily by tracked across multiple time frames to increase the accuracy of predictions. Candlestick patterns can be used in conjunction with other technical indicators such as moving averages, volume analysis and trend lines. Quantitative analysis is made easier, leading to the development of statistical models that quantify the probabilities associated with candlestick patterns.

Candlesticks and candlestick patterns have a rich history and have evolved over time. From their origins in 17th-century Japan to their widespread use in modern technical analysis, they have become an integral part of traders' toolkits. In today's fast-paced day trading markets, identifying and reacting to specific candlestick patterns rapidly can help assure a trader's success.

The Importance of Candlestick Patterns in Trading

Candlestick patterns are an essential tool in technical analysis for traders looking to make informed decisions in the financial markets. These patterns provide visual representations of price action, indicating shifts in market sentiment and potential trading opportunities. When applied to intraday trading , candlestick patterns can help identify short-term trends, reversals, and entry/exit points.

Candlestick patterns are formed by a combination of multiple candlesticks, each representing a specific time interval. The open, close, high and low prices of each interval are depicted through the body and wicks/shadows of the candlestick. By analyzing the relationships between these prices, traders can gain insights into market dynamics.

In intraday trading, where timeframes are relatively short, these charts provide detailed information about price movements within each interval. Traders can observe candlestick patterns forming in real-time and utilize them to make rapid trading decisions. When trading intraday it is crucial to understand candlestick patterns as they form so you can anticipate their continuation or reversal. Each pattern carries a specific meaning and can signal different market scenarios. Traders should look for patterns that align with their trading strategies and seek confirmation from other technical indicators. It's important to note that relying solely on candlestick patterns without additional analysis may lead to false signals.

Some momentum traders will use a chart with a short time frame, such as a one-minute chart, and often focus on patterns that provide timely insights. As the chart displays each minute's price action, it is possible to spot candlestick patterns forming. Traders often take advantage of these patterns to identify potential entry and exit points for quick trades.

Often, day traders will use a five-minute chart, which gives them more time to analyze patterns and make decisions. The patterns formed in this time frame may provide more reliable signals compared to the one-minute chart. Traders can still identify patterns quickly, but they may carry more weight due to the extended time frame. It is crucial to remain patient and not rush into trades solely based on one candlestick pattern. Regardless of the time frame, some common candlestick patterns include reversal patterns, continuation patterns, and indecision patterns. Reversal patterns signal potential trend reversals, while continuation patterns suggest the current trend is likely to continue. Indecision patterns often indicate a period of consolidation or market uncertainty.

When a candlestick pattern is identified, traders can use it to inform their trading decisions. For example, if a reversal patterns is recognized, such as a Bullish Engulfing pattern, it may indicate a potential bullish reversal. Traders could consider entering a long position or closing existing short positions, expecting the price to rise. However, it is important to wait for confirmation from subsequent candlesticks or other indicators before taking action.

Candlestick Patterns used with

Different Trading Styles

Long-term trading focuses on capturing significant price movements over weeks, months, or even years. Candlestick patterns can play a crucial role in analyzing the market behavior of long-term trading and providing insights into potential reversals, continuations, and trend confirmations. These patterns often offer clear signals and can provide valuable information for making informed long-term trading decisions. Some patterns that fall into this category include Marubozu, Hammer, Inverted Hammer, Engulfing, Bull Flag, and Morning Star.

Swing Trading is a style that aims to capture larger price swings over a few days to several weeks. Candlestick patterns are an important part of swing trading, providing valuable insights into market behavior and aiding in the identification of potential trend reversals, continuations, or breakouts. A Morning Star pattern that occurs at the end of a downtrend indicates a potential bullish reversal, making it valuable for swing traders looking for early indications of trend shifts.

Hammer and Inverted Hammer, characterized by small bodies and long shadows, suggest potential bullish reversals. Head and Shoulders, a long-term reversal pattern consisting of distinct peaks and troughs, is also well suited for swing trading. It indicates potential trend reversals and can help traders identify optimal entry or exit points.

Day Trading is a fast-paced intraday trading style that requires quick decision-making and capitalizing on short-term movements. Candlestick patterns are invaluable tools for day traders, providing insights into market behavior and aiding in the identification of profitable trading opportunities. As with any trading style, some candlestick patterns work better than others. Patterns that work best for day trading are those that offer clear and immediate signals, allowing traders to make rapid trading decisions. These patterns often indicate potential trend reversals, breakouts, or continuations, enabling day traders to capitalize on short-term price movements. Examples of patterns that work well for day trading include Engulfing, Morning Star, Hammer, Inverted Hammer, Bull Flag, Shooting Star, Bear Flat, Tweezer, and Head and Shoulders patterns.

Scalping is a popular short-term trading approach characterized by multiple quick trades throughout the day, aiming to capture small price differentials. In scalp trading, speed and precision are essential and traders rely on candlestick patterns that offer immediate signals and facilitate swift decision-making. Candlestick patterns play a vital role in scalping, providing valuable insights into market behavior and giving visual assistance in finding potential reversals, breakouts, or short-term price movements. Scalping is reliant on quick candlestick reading and tends to use smaller patterns, unlike other forms of trading. Candlestick patterns that scalping traders find useful include Engulfing, Hammer, Inverted Hammer, Doji, and Dragonfly.

This book includes 66 of the most useful patterns and quizzes to improve your identification and understanding of these candlestick patterns.

A Basic Candlestick

A basic candlestick represents the price action within a specific time frame, such as a minute, hour, or day. It consists of four main components: open, close, high, and low prices. The body of the candlestick represents the range between the open and close prices, while the wicks or shadows depict the high and low prices.

To trade a single candlestick on an intraday chart, it is important to consider the context and the specific type of candlestick formation. Different candlestick patterns provide insights into market sentiment and potential trading opportunities. For example, a bullish candlestick with a large body and small or nonexistent wicks suggests strong buying pressure. In this case, traders may consider entering a long position or holding onto existing long positions, anticipating further upward movement.

A bearish candlestick with a large body and minimal wicks indicates strong selling pressure. Traders might consider shorting the stock or closing existing long positions to take advantage of potential downward movement.

It is essential to remember that trading decisions should not rely solely on single candlestick formations. It's advisable to use candlestick patterns in conjunction with other indicators, such as moving averages, trendlines, and volume analysis, to confirm potential trade setups and manage risk effectively.

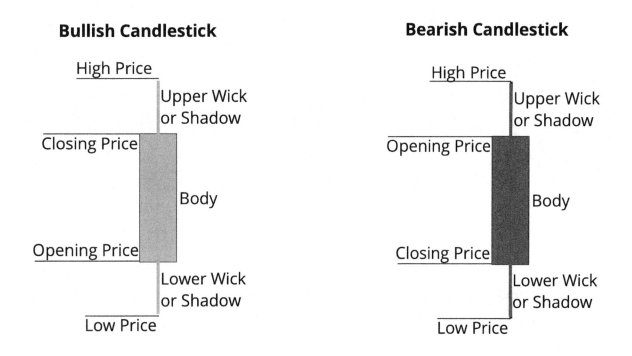

Bullish Candlestick

High Price
Upper Wick or Shadow
Closing Price
Body
Opening Price
Lower Wick or Shadow
Low Price

Bearish Candlestick

High Price
Upper Wick or Shadow
Opening Price
Body
Closing Price
Lower Wick or Shadow
Low Price

Candlestick Patterns are more Reliable with High Volume

The following are 5 candlestick pattern reference pages. The 66 candlestick patterns included are considered to be the trader's bible of analysis. The most common of these are included in the puzzles and challenges in this book.

Candlestick Patterns

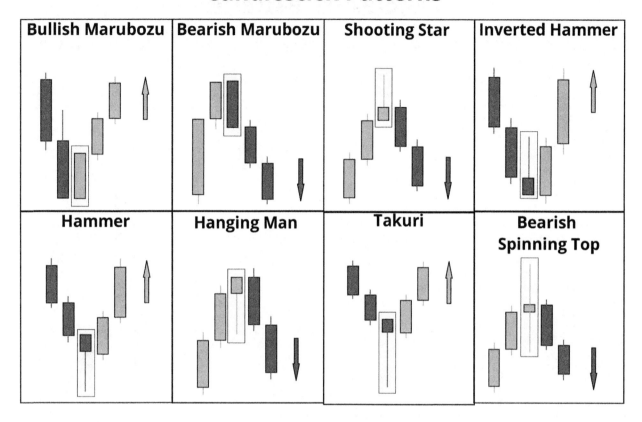

Bullish Marubozu	Bearish Marubozu	Shooting Star	Inverted Hammer
Hammer	**Hanging Man**	**Takuri**	**Bearish Spinning Top**

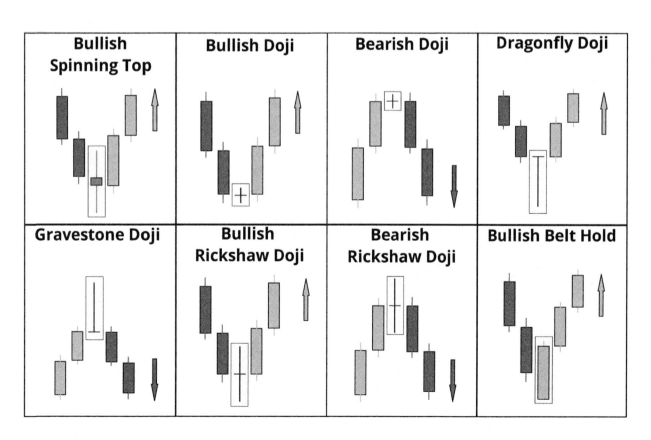

Bullish Spinning Top	Bullish Doji	Bearish Doji	Dragonfly Doji
Gravestone Doji	**Bullish Rickshaw Doji**	**Bearish Rickshaw Doji**	**Bullish Belt Hold**

Candlestick Patterns

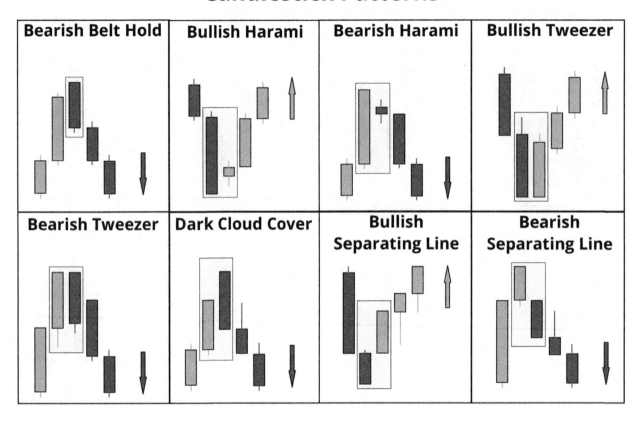

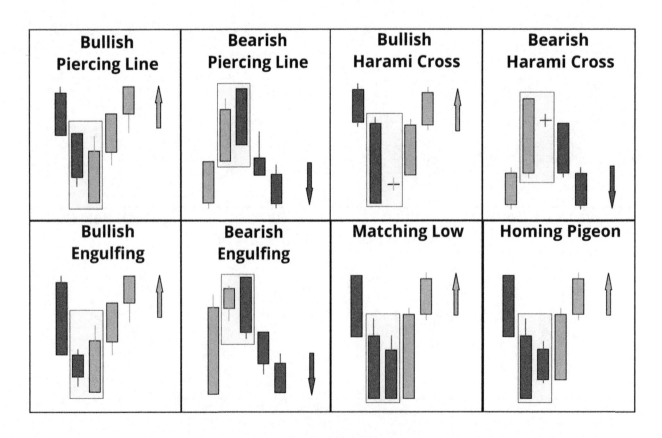

Candlestick Patterns

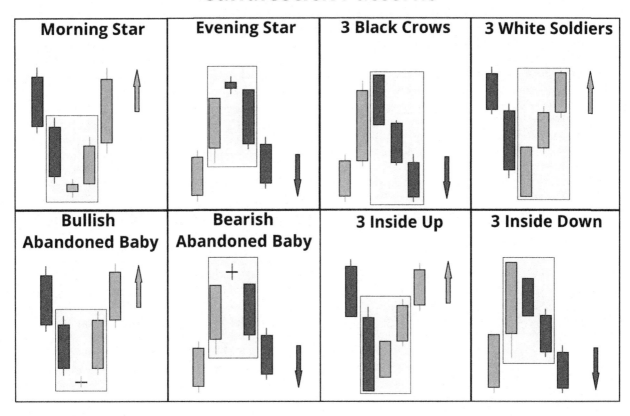

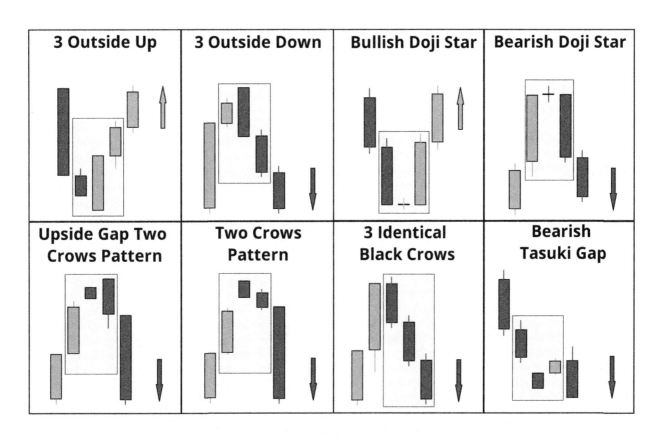

Candlestick Patterns

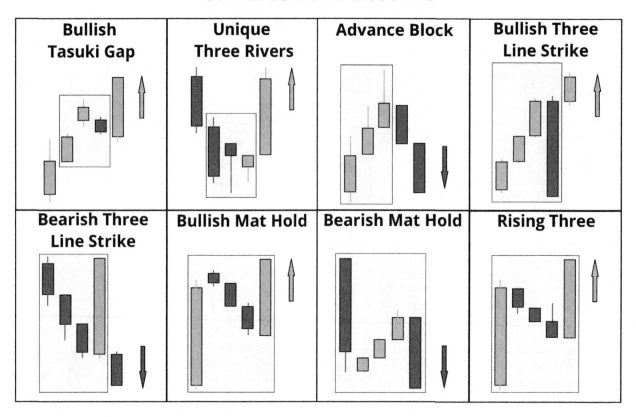

Bullish Tasuki Gap · Unique Three Rivers · Advance Block · Bullish Three Line Strike

Bearish Three Line Strike · Bullish Mat Hold · Bearish Mat Hold · Rising Three

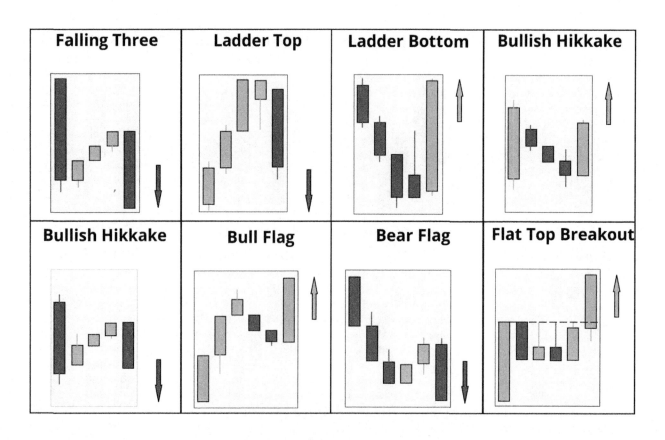

Falling Three · Ladder Top · Ladder Bottom · Bullish Hikkake

Bullish Hikkake · Bull Flag · Bear Flag · Flat Top Breakout

Candlestick Patterns

Head and Shoulders

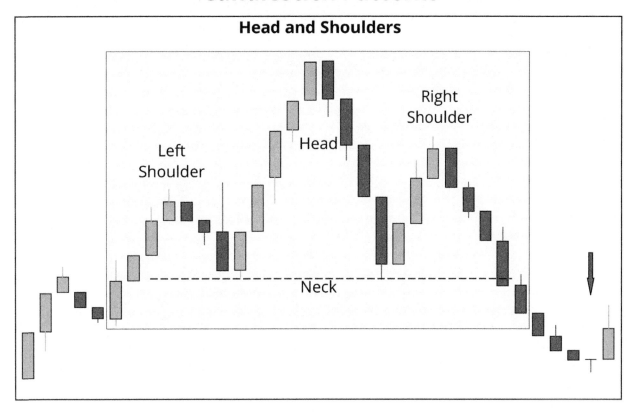

Left Shoulder

Head

Right Shoulder

Neck

Cup and Handle

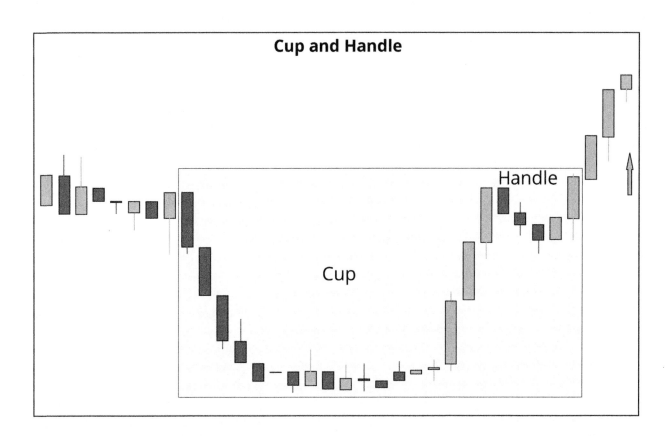

Handle

Cup

Chapter 2

Beginner Challenge

Find the Named Candlestick Pattern

within the Charts

Find the Named Candlestick Patterns

Within the following charts are common candlestick patterns. You can mark your answers in pencil or make a mental note and check your solutions so that you can repeat the challenge to improve your accuracy until you're 100% successful. It is important to note some of these patterns were originally identified for daily chart use only. The challenges have been adapted for intraday use based on their accuracy within 1- 5- 10- 15-minute charts. Professional traders found most daily candlestick patterns are useful within intraday charts of various time increments with certain allowances. When live trading, always be prepared to exit your position if the pattern is not reacting as predicted.

Give yourself bonus points if you correctly identify any patterns that are not in the answer pages in chapter 3

| Quiz number | Candlestick patterns to look for in this quiz |

| Quiz # | Bearish Tweezer, Shooting Star, Bearish Spinning Top, Dragonfly, Bearish Doji, Bearish Rickshaw Man |

Candlestick chart

Quiz 1	**Bearish Tweezer, Shooting Star, Bearish Spinning Top, Dragonfly, Bearish Doji, Bearish Rickshaw Man**

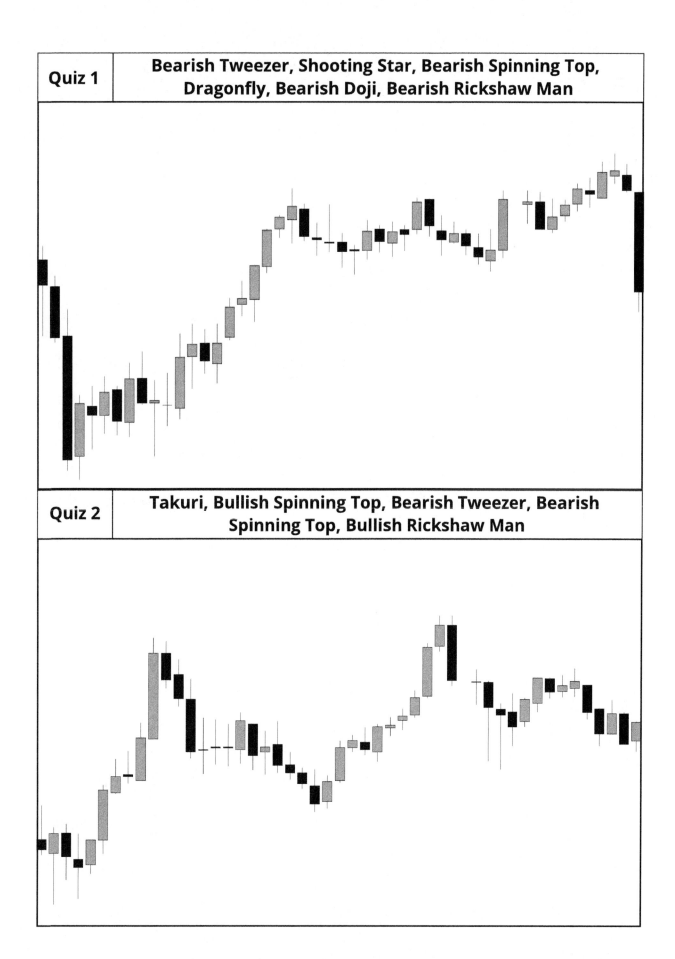

Quiz 2	**Takuri, Bullish Spinning Top, Bearish Tweezer, Bearish Spinning Top, Bullish Rickshaw Man**

Quiz 3	Shooting Star, Gravestone, Bullish Tweezer, Bullish Spinning Top, Bearish Tweezer, Takuri

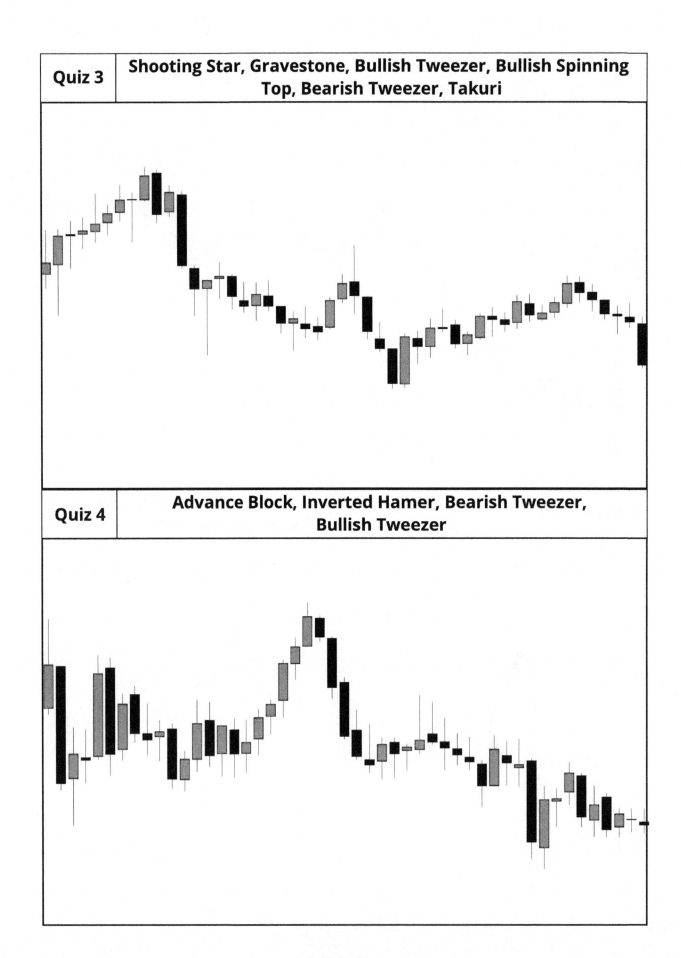

Quiz 4	Advance Block, Inverted Hamer, Bearish Tweezer, Bullish Tweezer

Quiz 5	Inverted Hammer, Bearish Harami, Bearish Spinning Top, Bearish Tweezer, Bullish Spinning Top, Bearish Hikkake

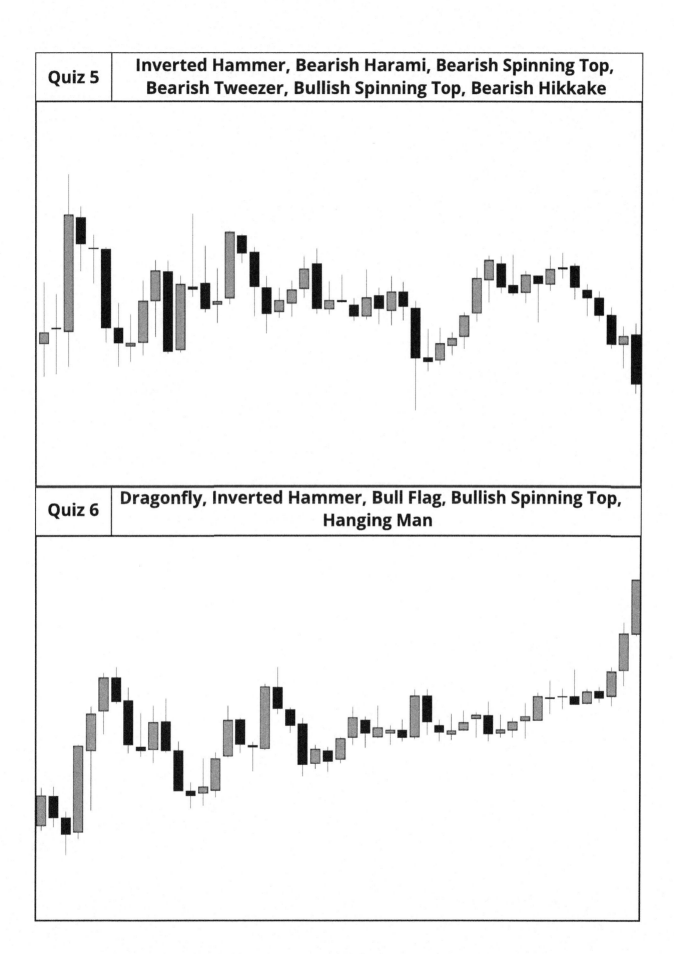

Quiz 6	Dragonfly, Inverted Hammer, Bull Flag, Bullish Spinning Top, Hanging Man

Quiz 7	Bear Flag, Gravestone, Bullish Tweezer

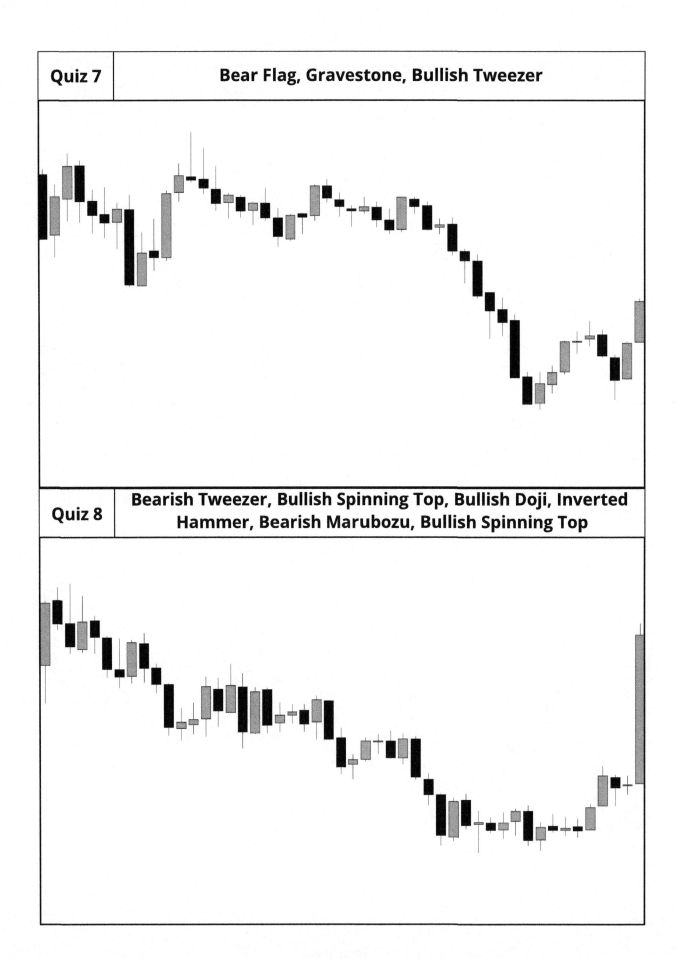

Quiz 8	Bearish Tweezer, Bullish Spinning Top, Bullish Doji, Inverted Hammer, Bearish Marubozu, Bullish Spinning Top

Quiz 9	Hammer, Bullish Spinning Top, Shooting Star, Bearish Tweezer, Bull Flag, Bullish Tweezer

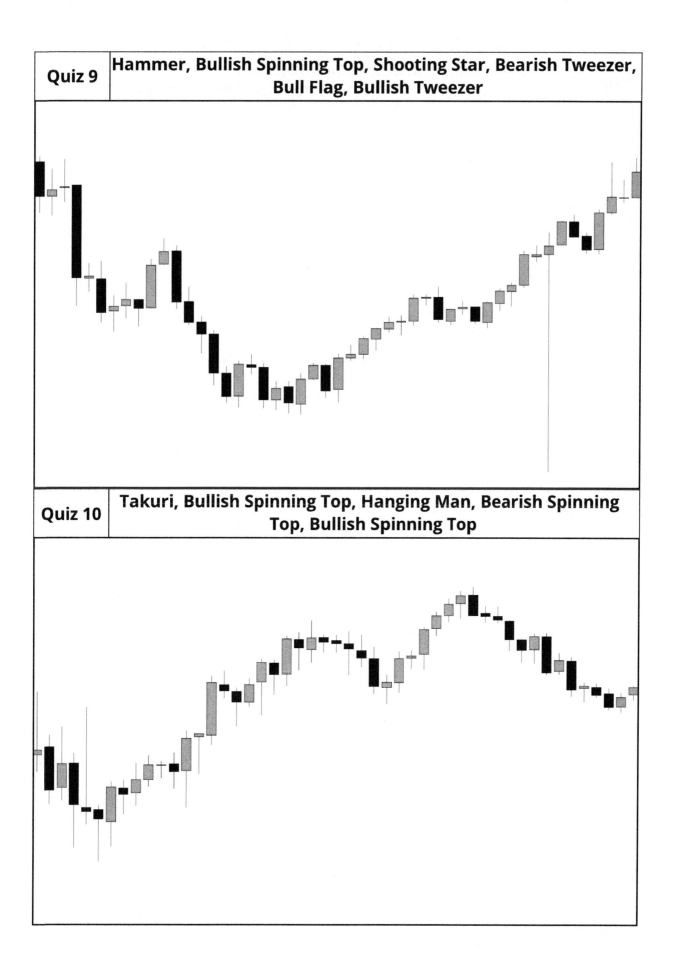

Quiz 10	Takuri, Bullish Spinning Top, Hanging Man, Bearish Spinning Top, Bullish Spinning Top

Quiz 11	**Bear Flag, Bullish Spinning Top, Advance Block, Bearish Spinning Top, Bearish Tweezer, Bullish Tweezer**

Quiz 12	**Hammer, Bearish Rickshaw Man, Flat Top Breakout, Bearish Rickshaw Man, Bullish Spinning Top**

Quiz 13	**Bull Flag, Hammer, Hanging Man, Bullish Spinning Top, Dragonfly, Gravestone**

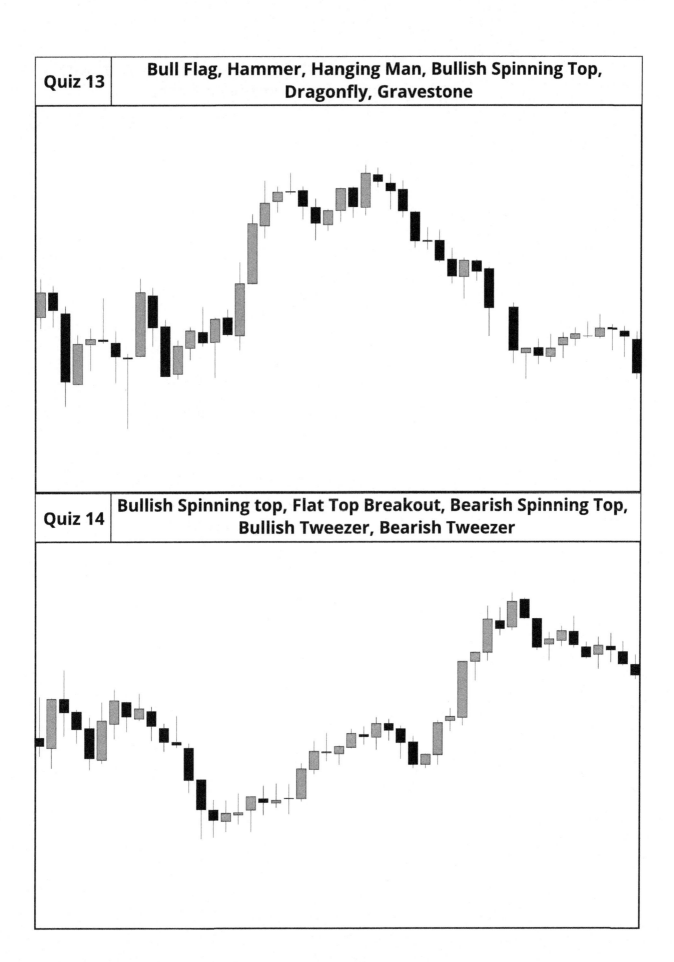

Quiz 14	**Bullish Spinning top, Flat Top Breakout, Bearish Spinning Top, Bullish Tweezer, Bearish Tweezer**

Quiz 15	Takuri, Shooting Star, Bearish Marubozu, Bullish Tweezer, Bearish Tweezer, Inverted Hammer

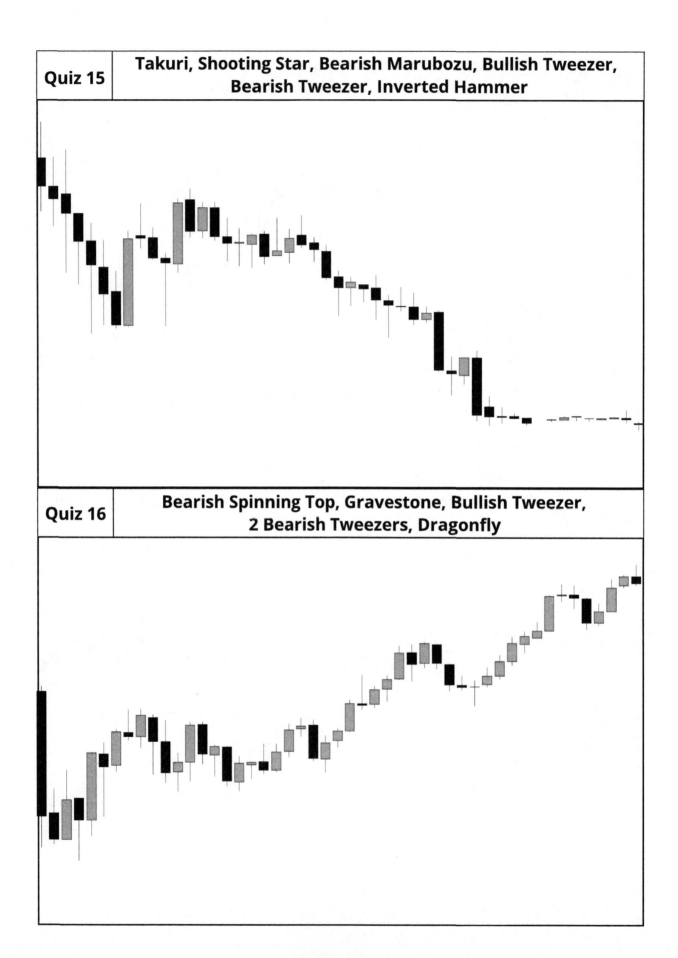

Quiz 16	Bearish Spinning Top, Gravestone, Bullish Tweezer, 2 Bearish Tweezers, Dragonfly

Quiz 17	**Bullish Tweezer, Bearish Tweezer, Bullish Spinning Top, Bearish Spinning Top, Three White Soldiers, Hammer**

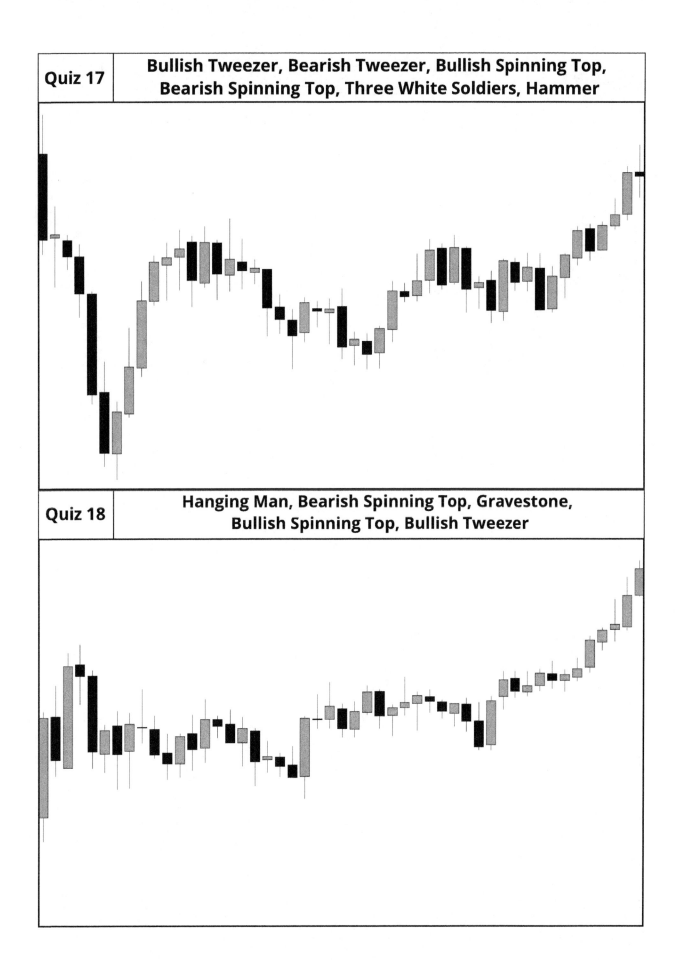

Quiz 18	**Hanging Man, Bearish Spinning Top, Gravestone, Bullish Spinning Top, Bullish Tweezer**

Quiz 19	**Bearish Rickshaw Man, Takuri, Bullish Doji, Hanging Man, Bearish Tweezer, Bullish Doji**

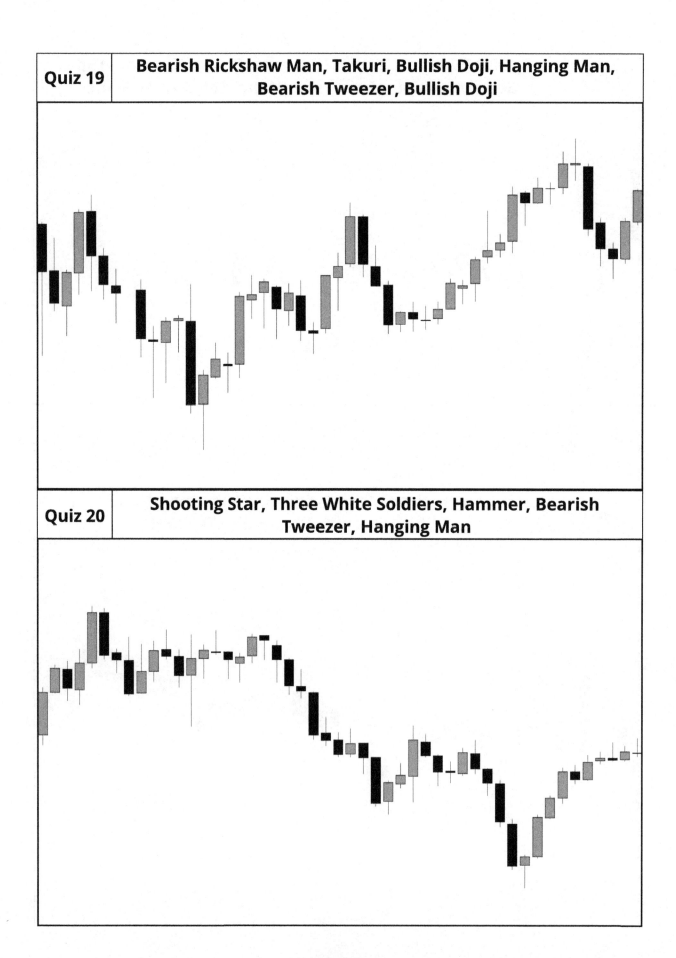

Quiz 20	**Shooting Star, Three White Soldiers, Hammer, Bearish Tweezer, Hanging Man**

Quiz 21	Bullish Doji, 2 Bearish Tweezer, Three White Soldiers, Gravestone, Bullish Tweezer

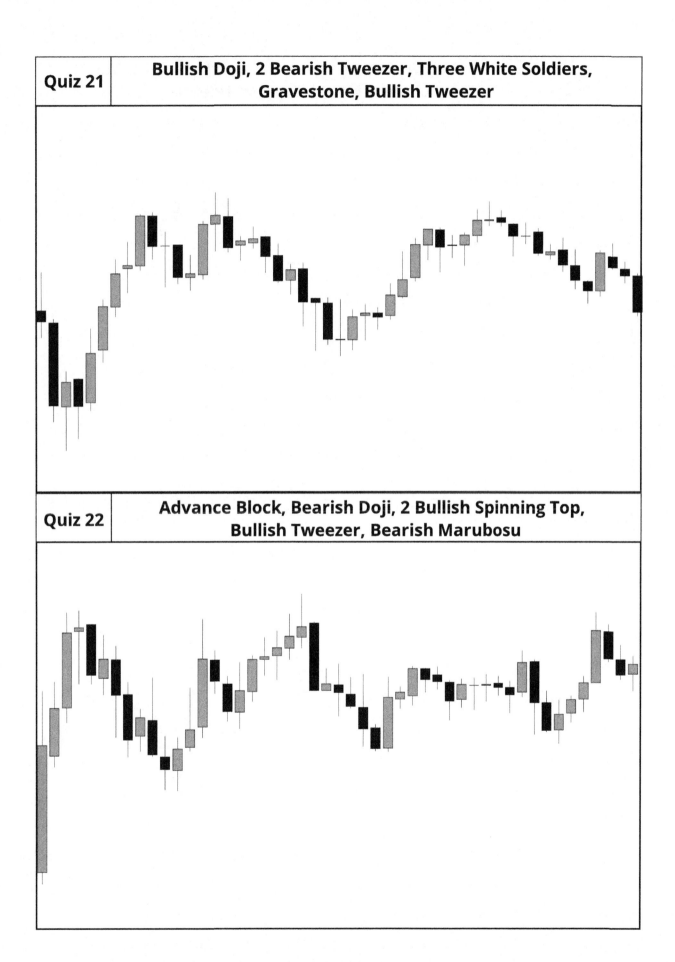

Quiz 22	Advance Block, Bearish Doji, 2 Bullish Spinning Top, Bullish Tweezer, Bearish Marubosu

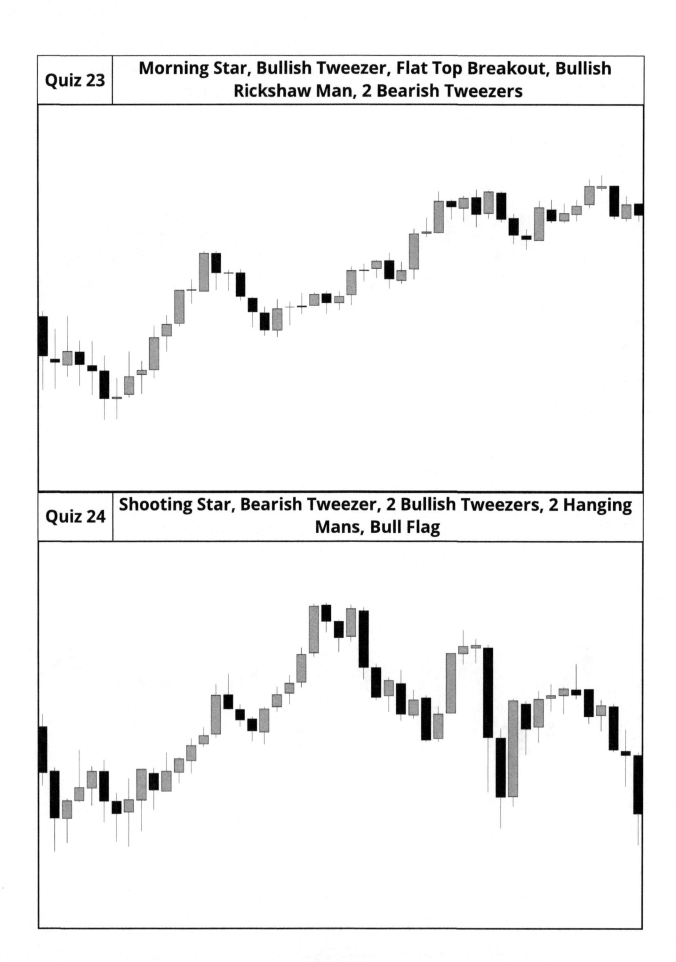

Quiz 23	**Morning Star, Bullish Tweezer, Flat Top Breakout, Bullish Rickshaw Man, 2 Bearish Tweezers**

Quiz 24	**Shooting Star, Bearish Tweezer, 2 Bullish Tweezers, 2 Hanging Mans, Bull Flag**

Quiz 25	**Bullish Marubosu, Flat Top Breakout, Bullish Spinning Top, Bearish Doji, Bullish Harami**

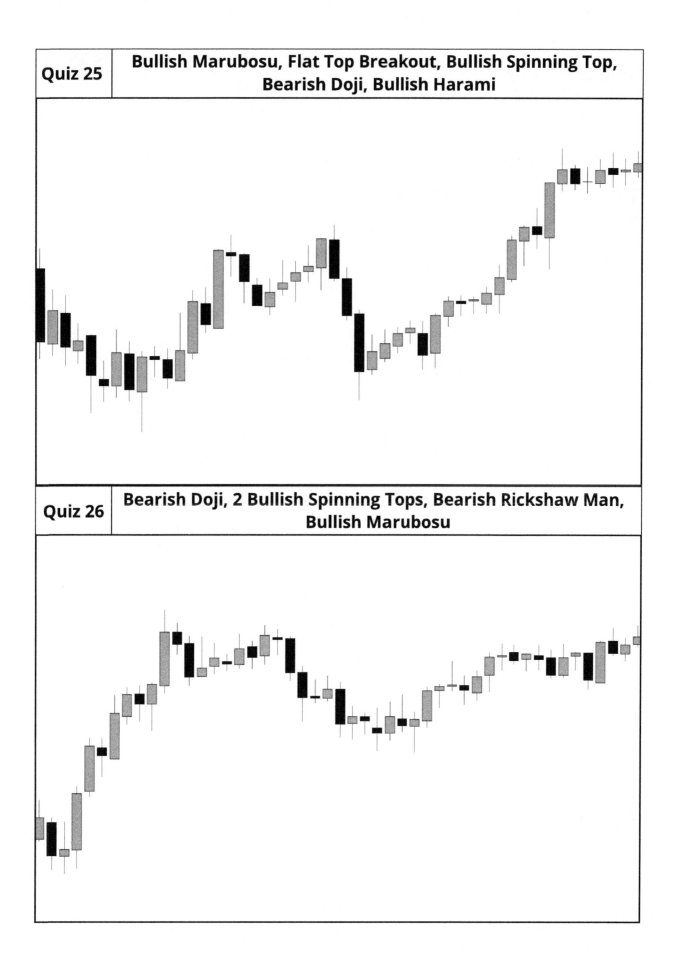

Quiz 26	**Bearish Doji, 2 Bullish Spinning Tops, Bearish Rickshaw Man, Bullish Marubosu**

Quiz 27	**Dragonfly, Three Black Crows, Bullish Tweezer, Dragonfly, Takuri**

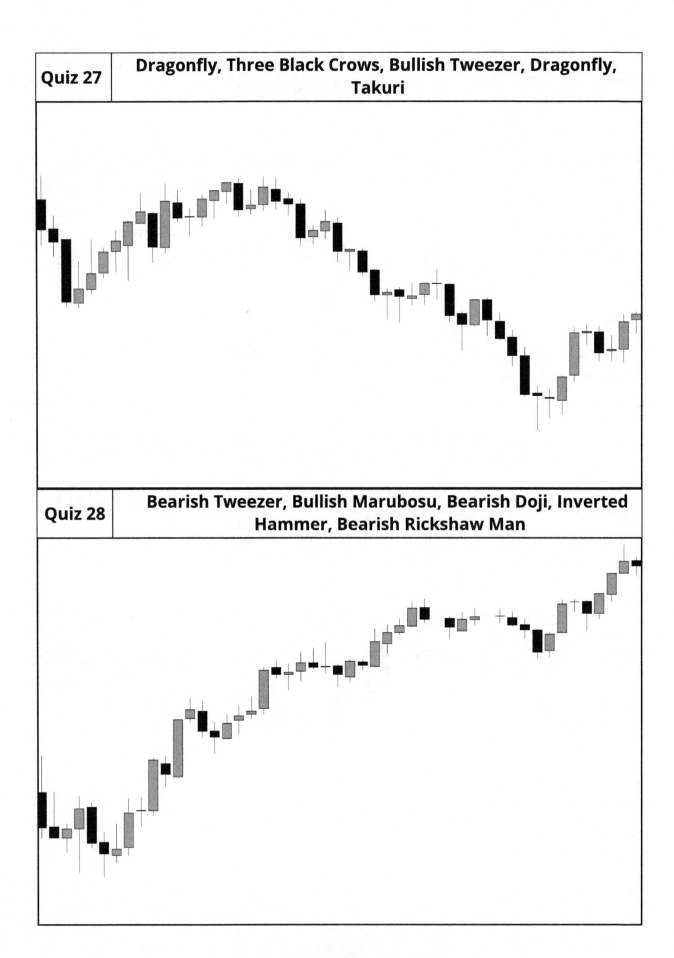

Quiz 28	**Bearish Tweezer, Bullish Marubosu, Bearish Doji, Inverted Hammer, Bearish Rickshaw Man**

Quiz 29	**Bullish Tweezer, Hanging Man, 2 Hammers, Bearish Tweezer**

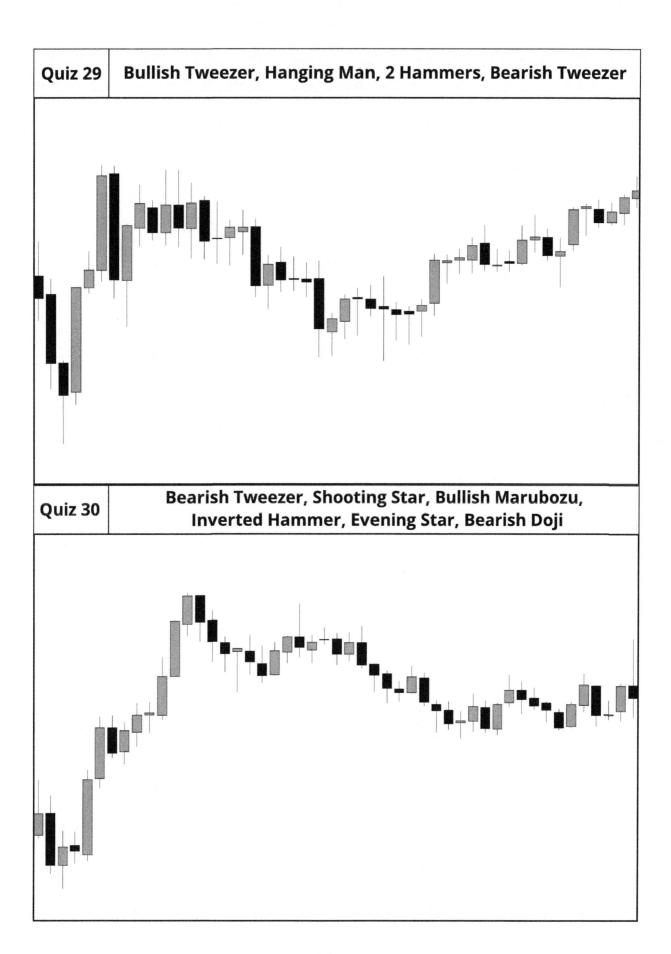

Quiz 30	**Bearish Tweezer, Shooting Star, Bullish Marubozu, Inverted Hammer, Evening Star, Bearish Doji**

Quiz 31	Inverted Hammer, Bullish Spinning Top, Bullish Tweezer, Three White Soldiers, Hanging Man

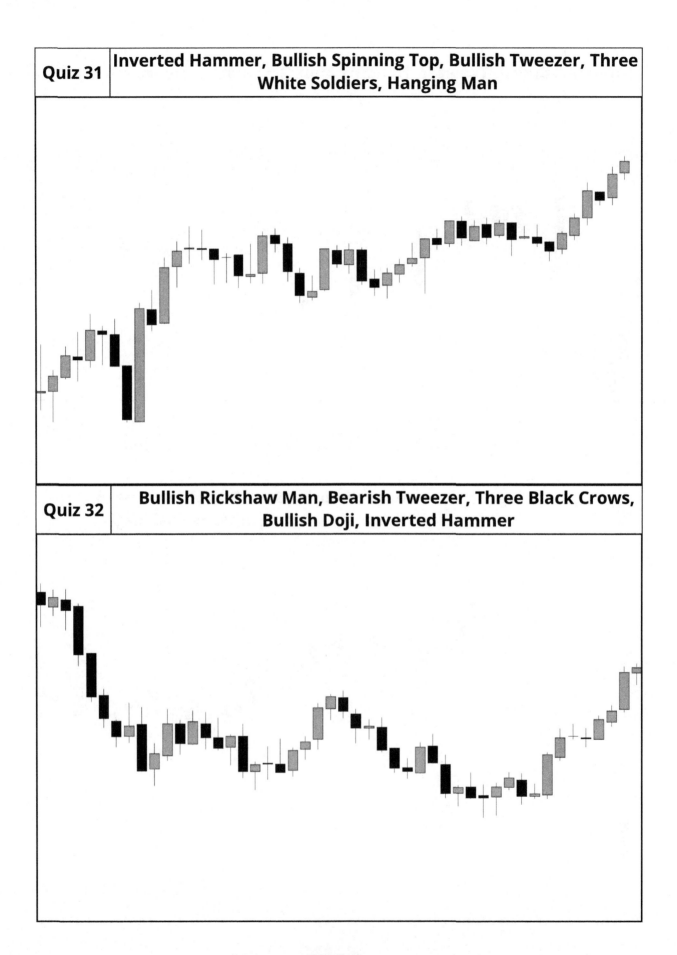

Quiz 32	Bullish Rickshaw Man, Bearish Tweezer, Three Black Crows, Bullish Doji, Inverted Hammer

Quiz 33	Three White Soldiers, Bear Flag, Dragonfly, Bullish Tweezer, Bearish Spinng Top

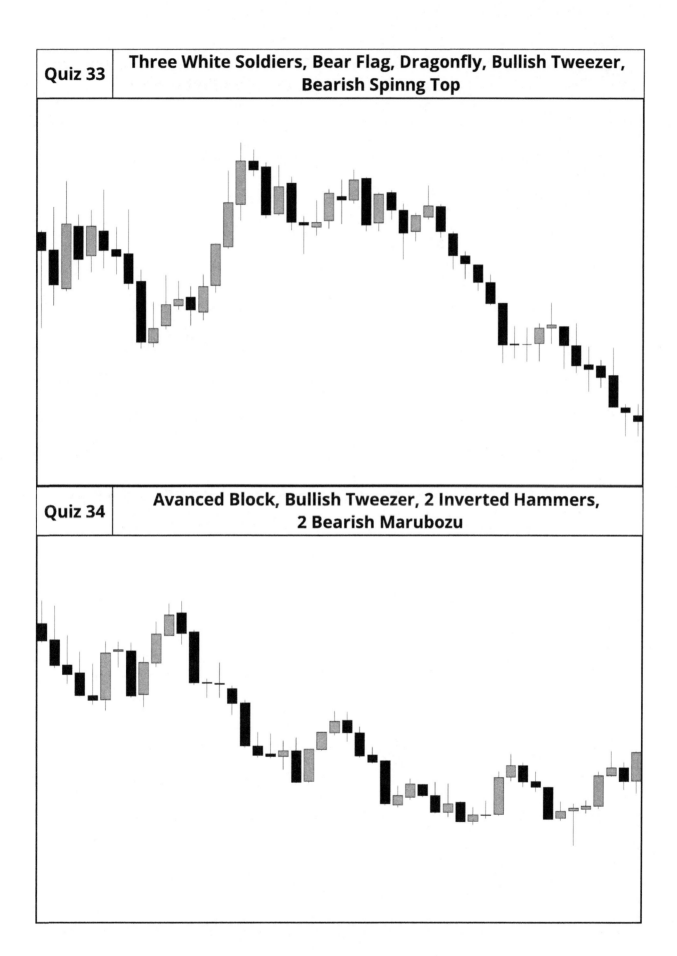

Quiz 34	Avanced Block, Bullish Tweezer, 2 Inverted Hammers, 2 Bearish Marubozu

Quiz 35	Bear Flag, Bullish Doji, Bullish Tweezer, and Bearish Marubozu candlestick patterns. Can you find them?

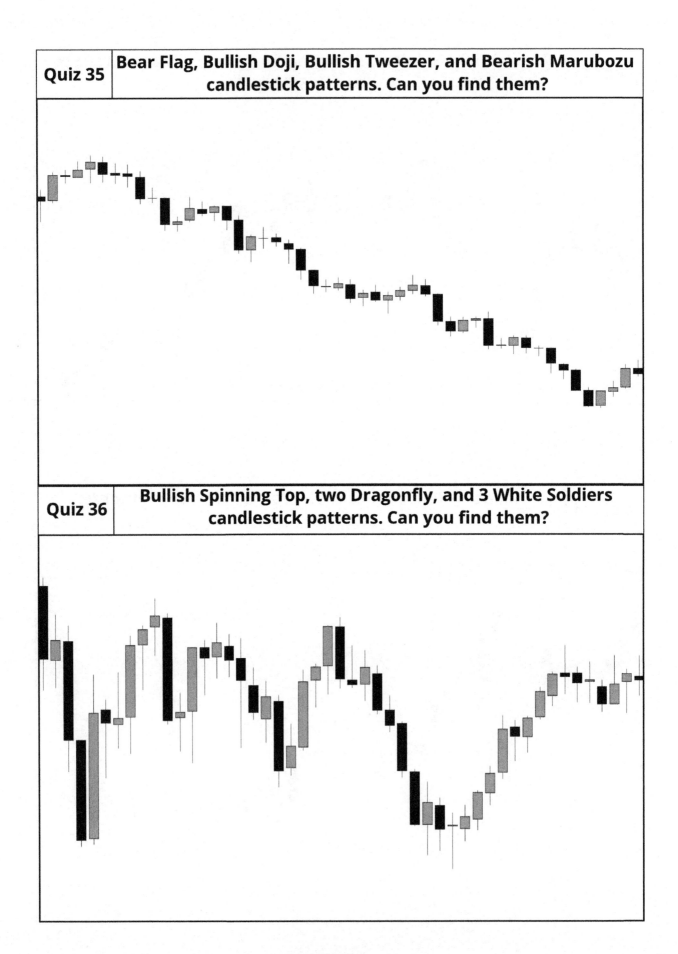

Quiz 36	Bullish Spinning Top, two Dragonfly, and 3 White Soldiers candlestick patterns. Can you find them?

Quiz 37	**Shooting Star, Bearish Doji, Bearish Tweezer, Bullish Spinning Top, Bullish Tweezer**

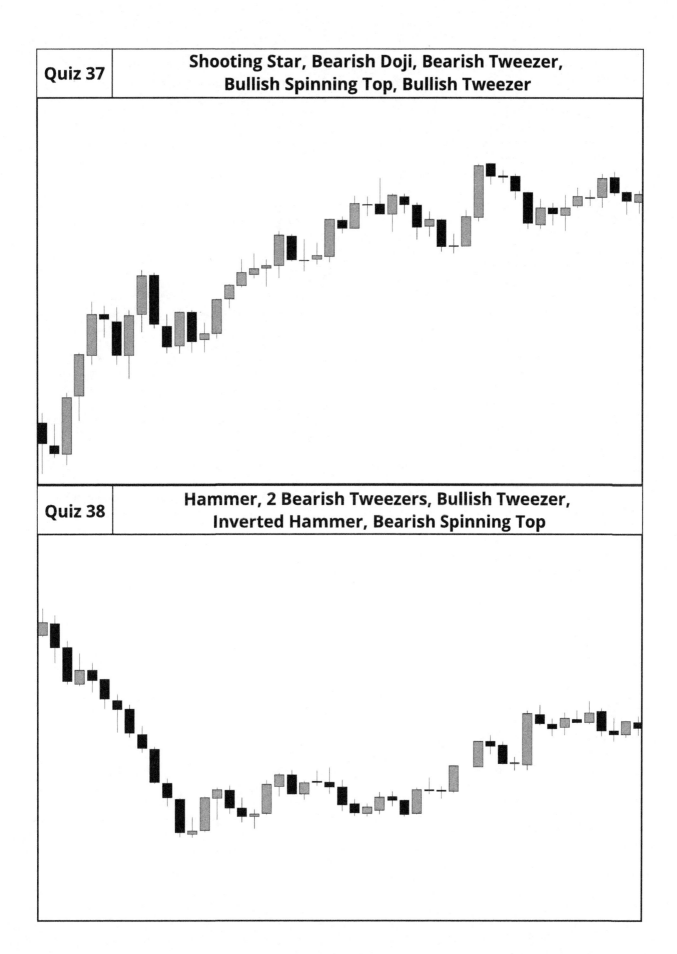

Quiz 38	**Hammer, 2 Bearish Tweezers, Bullish Tweezer, Inverted Hammer, Bearish Spinning Top**

Quiz 39	**Bearish Tweezer, Hanging Man, 2 Bullish Spinning Tops, Engulfing Candle, Bearish Tweezer**

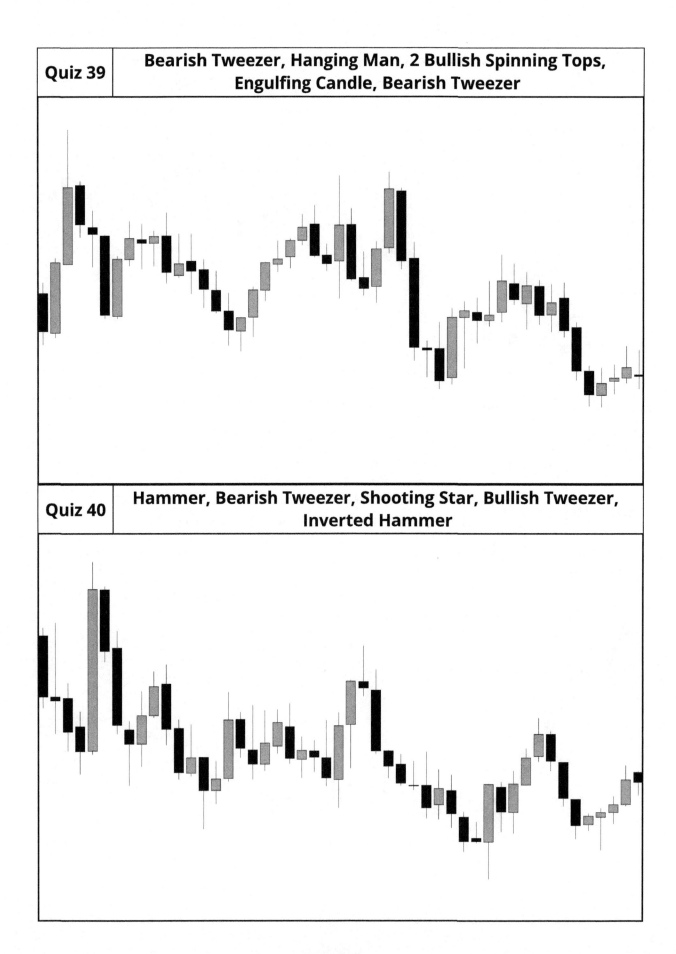

Quiz 40	**Hammer, Bearish Tweezer, Shooting Star, Bullish Tweezer, Inverted Hammer**

Quiz 41	**Flat Top Breakout, Hammer, 2 Bearish Tweezers, Bullish Tweezer**

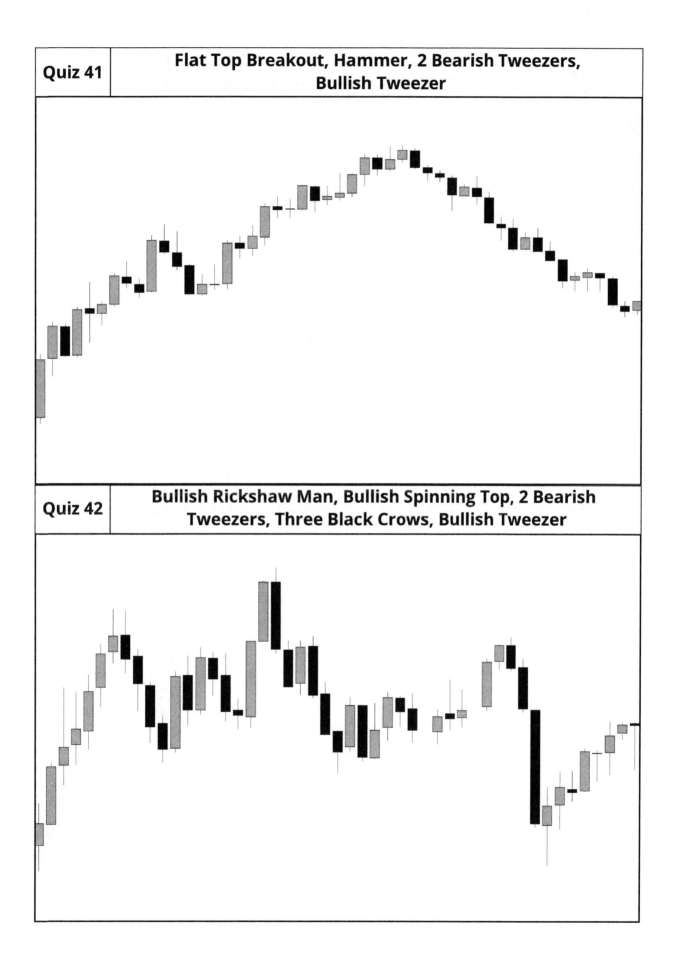

Quiz 42	**Bullish Rickshaw Man, Bullish Spinning Top, 2 Bearish Tweezers, Three Black Crows, Bullish Tweezer**

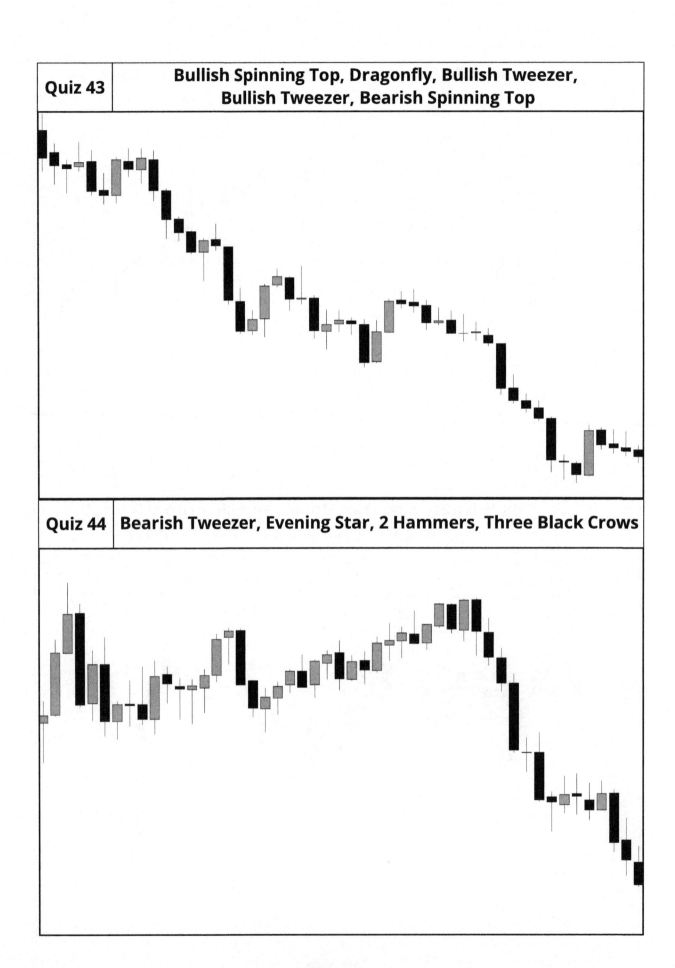

| Quiz 43 | Bullish Spinning Top, Dragonfly, Bullish Tweezer, Bullish Tweezer, Bearish Spinning Top |

| Quiz 44 | Bearish Tweezer, Evening Star, 2 Hammers, Three Black Crows |

Quiz 45	Takuri, Dragonfly, Gravestone, Tweezer, Bullish Tweezer, Hammer, Bearish Spinning Top

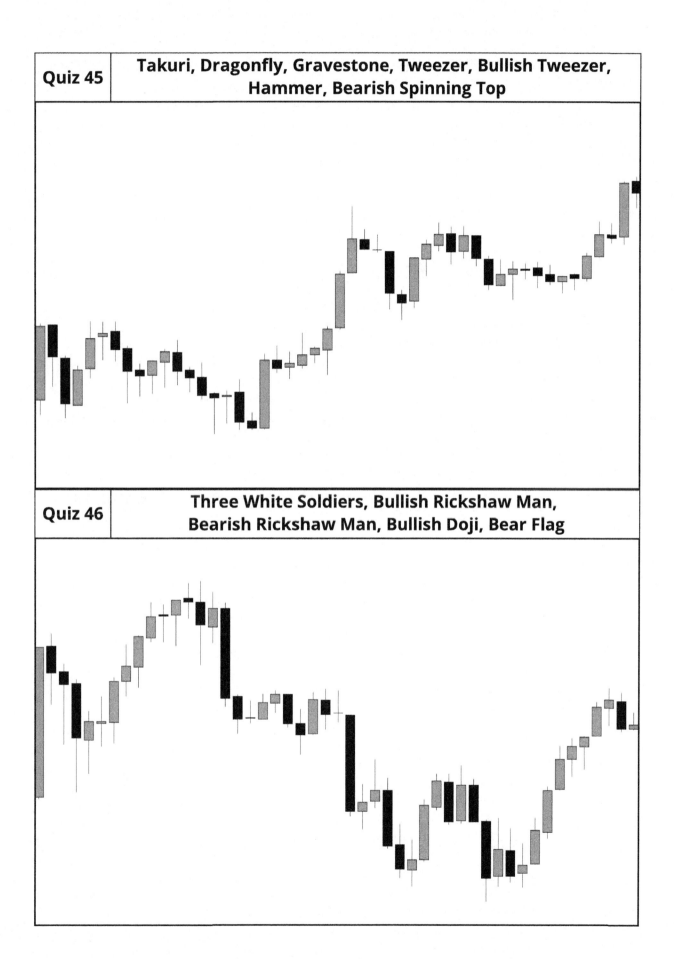

Quiz 46	Three White Soldiers, Bullish Rickshaw Man, Bearish Rickshaw Man, Bullish Doji, Bear Flag

Quiz 47	Shooting Star, Hanging Man, Bull Flag, Dragonfly, Gravestone, Hammer

Quiz 48	Bull Flag, Bear Flag, 2 Shooting Stars, Bearish Marubosu, Inverted Hammer

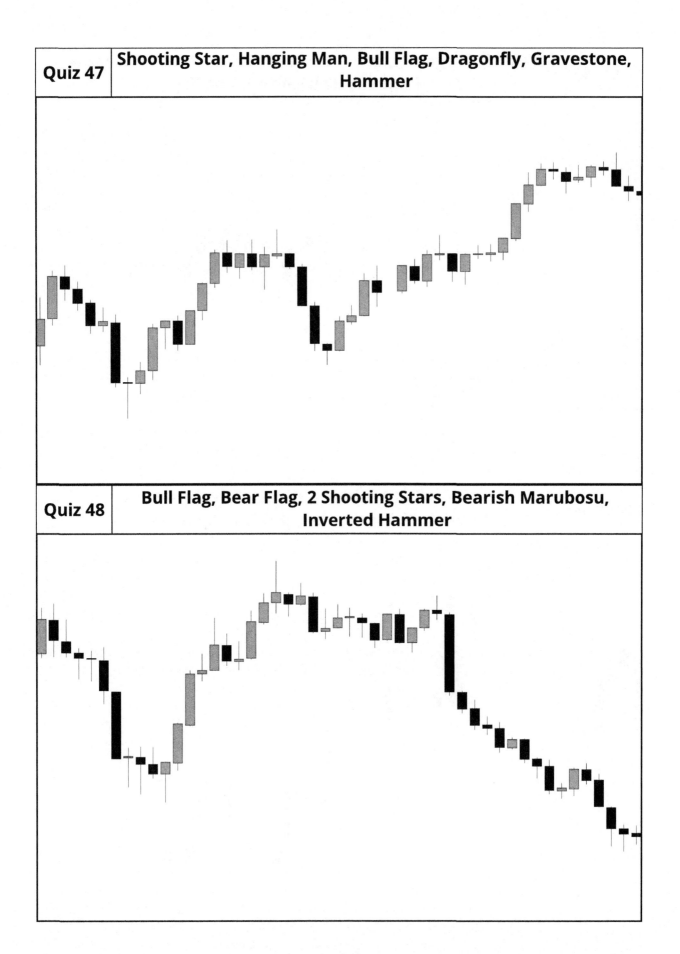

Quiz 49	**Bearish Tweezer, Inverted Hammer, Three Black Crows, Hammer, Shooting Star**

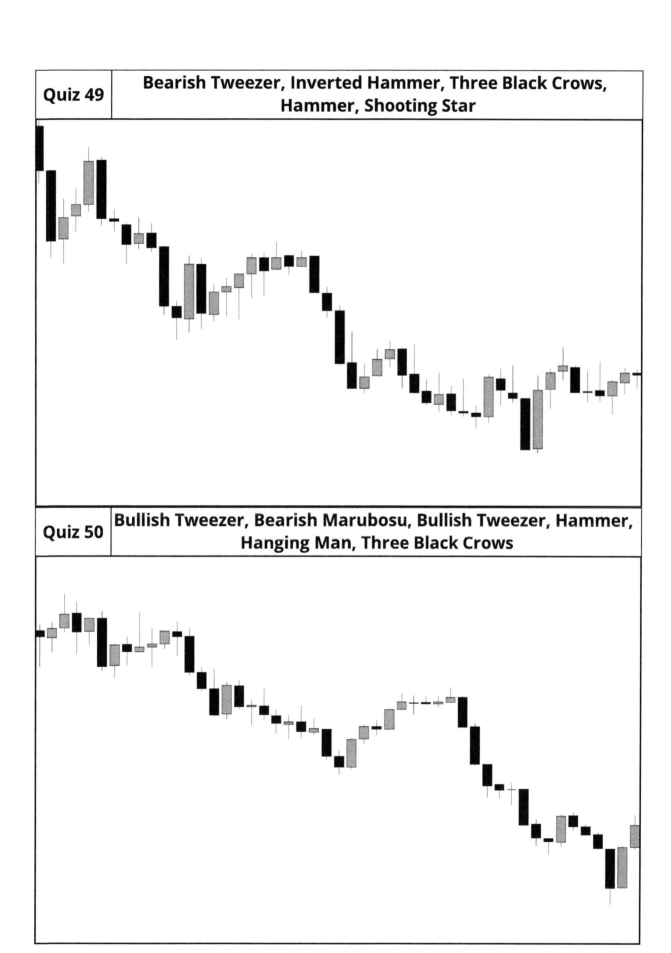

Quiz 50	**Bullish Tweezer, Bearish Marubosu, Bullish Tweezer, Hammer, Hanging Man, Three Black Crows**

Chapter 3

Answers for Beginner Challenge

Answers for Beginner Challenge

The pages that follow contain the answers for the beginner challenge. The goal was to identify all the candlestick patterns you found by marking or noting them. Repeat the test until achieving 100% accuracy. Don't forget give yourself extra credit if you identified any other patterns. Take your time on this challenge exploring and mastering the art of recognizing candlestick patterns. This is your first step to becoming a better trader.

Number of the Quiz	#'s and names of the Candlestick Pattern
Quiz # Answers	1 Bearish Spinning Top, 2 Dragon Fly, 3 Bearish Tweezer, 4 Bearish Rickshaw Man, 5 Bullish Doji, 6 Shooting Star

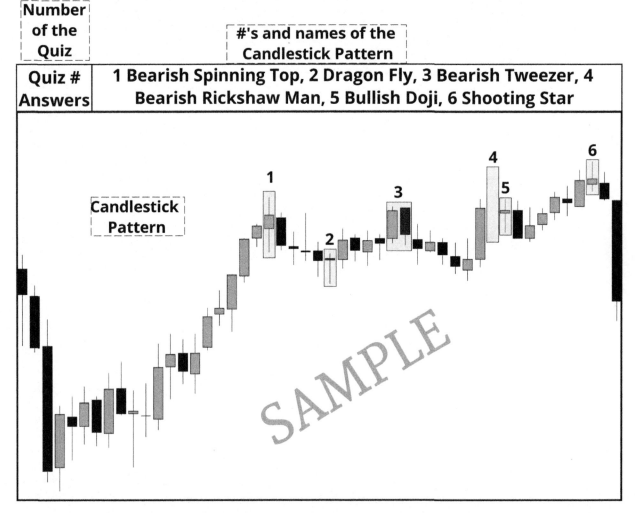

Quiz 1 Answers	1 Bearish Spinning Top, 2 Dragon Fly, 3 Bearish Tweezer, 4 Bearish Rickshaw Man, 5 Bearish Doji, 6 Shooting Star

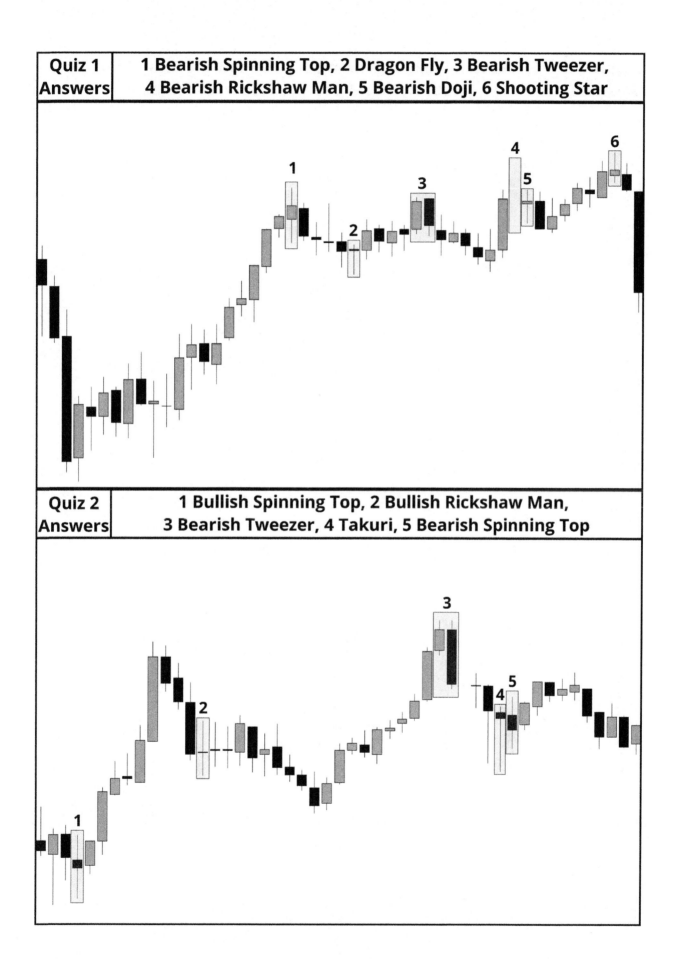

Quiz 2 Answers	1 Bullish Spinning Top, 2 Bullish Rickshaw Man, 3 Bearish Tweezer, 4 Takuri, 5 Bearish Spinning Top

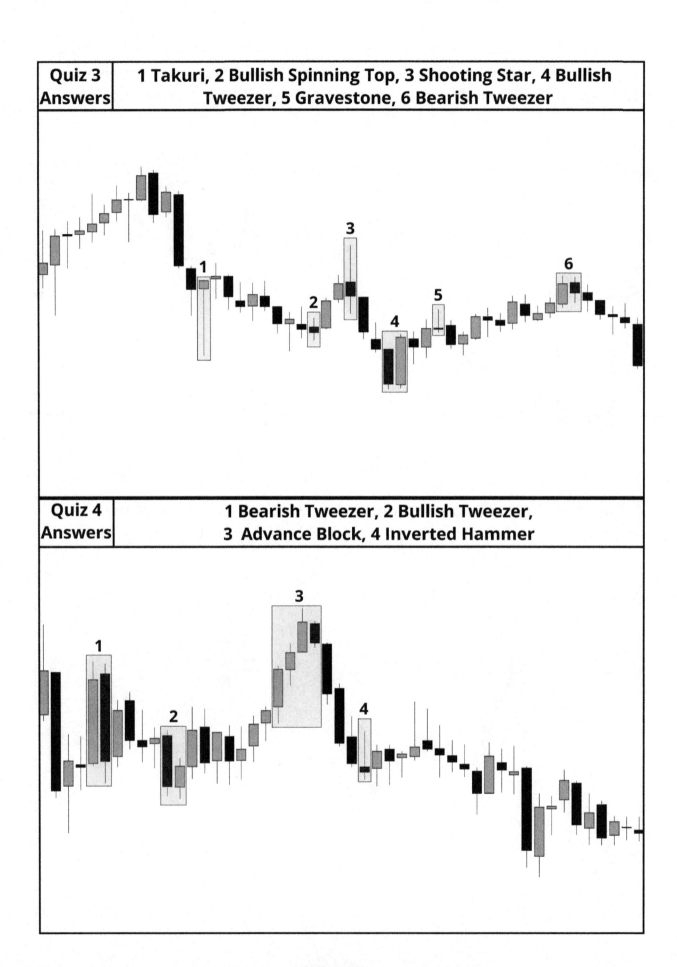

Quiz 3 Answers	1 Takuri, 2 Bullish Spinning Top, 3 Shooting Star, 4 Bullish Tweezer, 5 Gravestone, 6 Bearish Tweezer

Quiz 4 Answers	1 Bearish Tweezer, 2 Bullish Tweezer, 3 Advance Block, 4 Inverted Hammer

Quiz 5 Answers	1 Bullish Spinning Top, 2 Bearish Tweezer, 3 Bearish Harami, 4 Bearish Hikkake, 5 Inverted Hammer, 6 Bearish Spinning Top

Quiz 6 Answers	1 Bull Flag, 2 Bullish Spinning Top, 3 Dragonfly, 4 Hanging Man, 5 Inverted Hammer

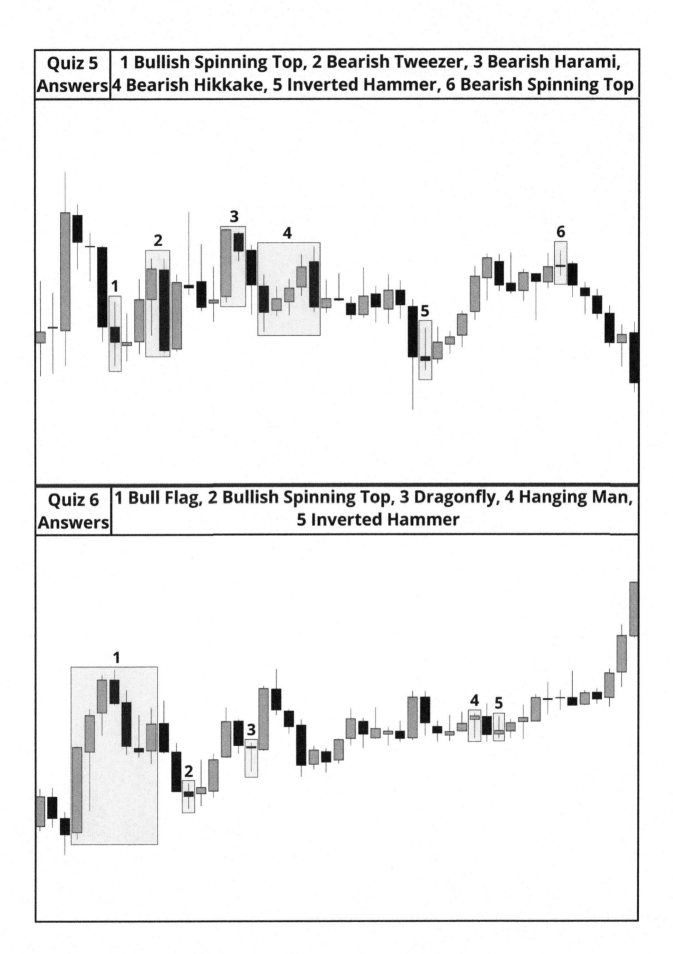

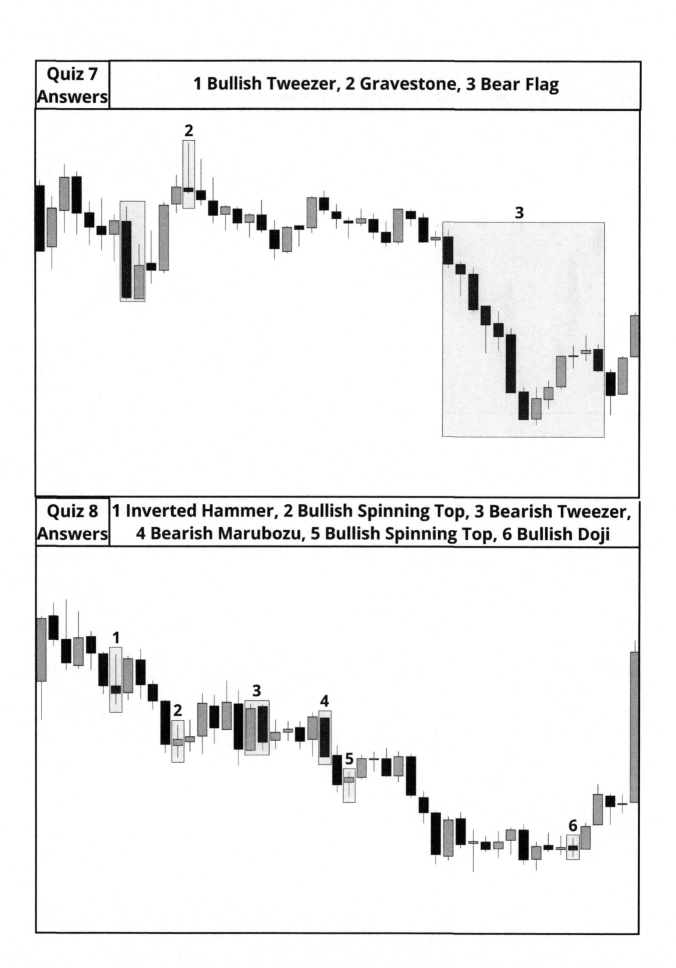

Quiz 7 Answers	1 Bullish Tweezer, 2 Gravestone, 3 Bear Flag

Quiz 8 Answers	1 Inverted Hammer, 2 Bullish Spinning Top, 3 Bearish Tweezer, 4 Bearish Marubozu, 5 Bullish Spinning Top, 6 Bullish Doji

Quiz 9 Answers	1 Shooting Star, 2 Bullish Spinning Top, 3 Hammer, 4 Bearish Tweezer, 5 Bullish Tweezer, 6 Bull Flag

Quiz 10 Answers	1 Takuri, 2 Bearish Spinning Top, 3 Bullish Spinning Top, 4 Hanging Man, 5 Bullish Spinning Top

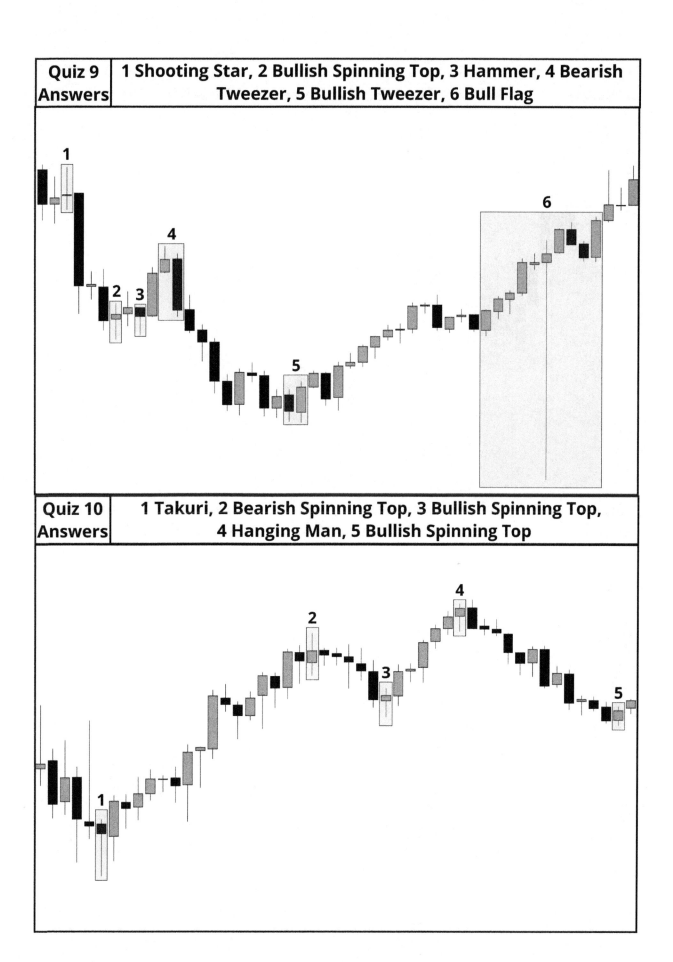

Quiz 11 Answers	1 Advance Block, 2 Bearish Spinning Top, 3 Bear Flag, 4 Bullish Spining Top, 5 Bullish Tweezer, 6 Bearish Tweezer

Quiz 12 Answers	1 Bearish Rickshaw Man, 2 Flat Top Breakout, 3 Hammer, 4 Bearish Rickshaw Man, 5 Bullish Spinning Top

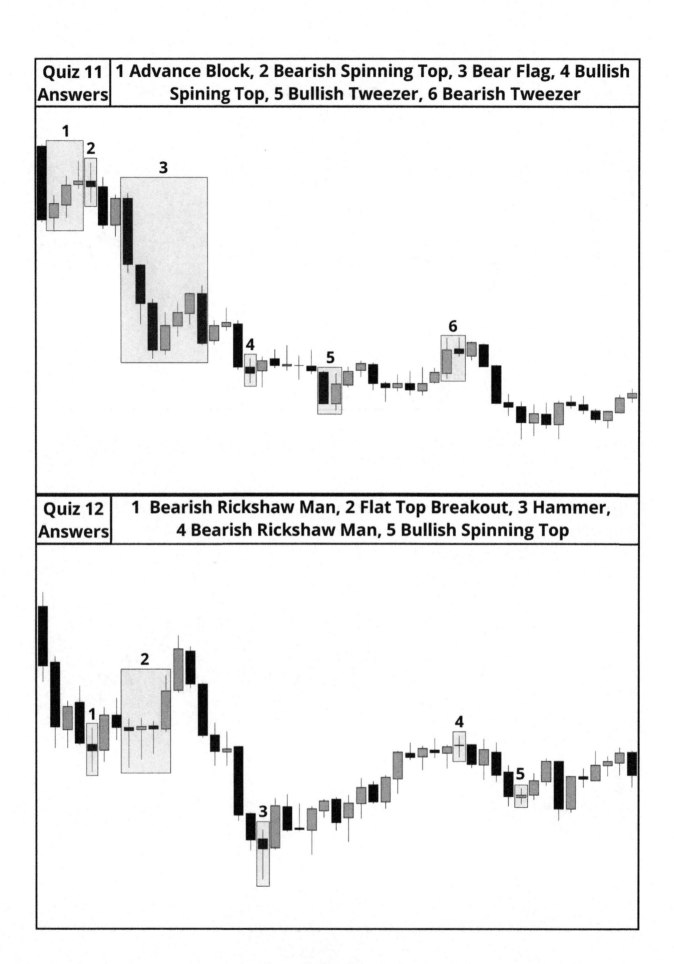

Quiz 13 Answers	1 Gravestone, 2 Dragonfly, 3 Bullish Tweezer, 4 Bull Flag, 5 Hammer, 6 Bullish Spinning Top, 7 Hanging Man

Quiz 14 Answers	1 Bearish Spinning Top, 2 Bullish Spinning Top, 3 Flat Top Breakout, 4 Bearish Tweezer, 5 Bullish Tweezer

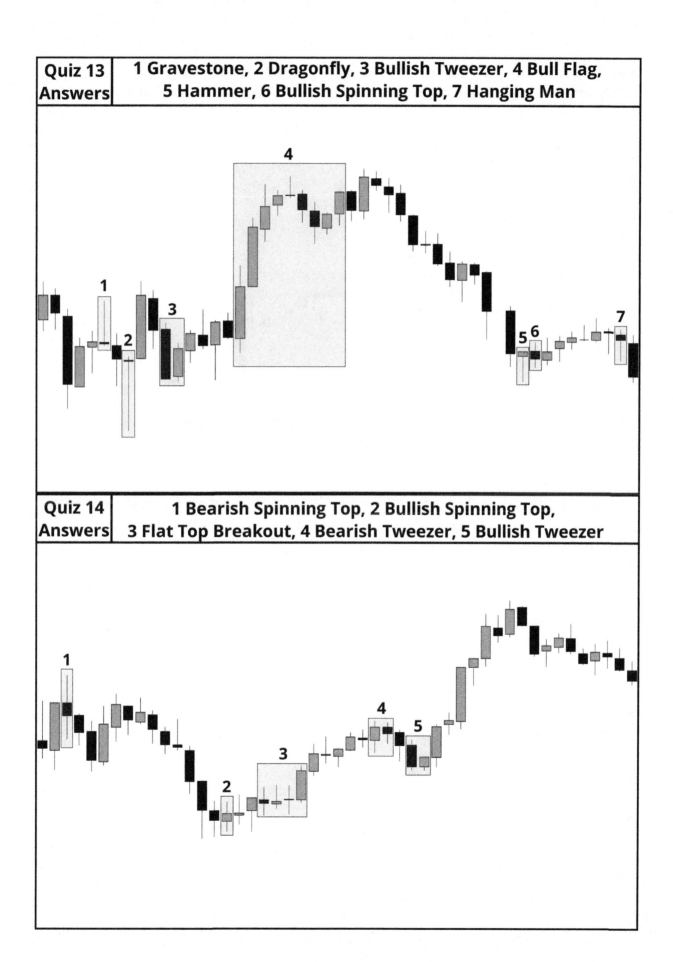

Quiz 15 Answers	1 Bullish Tweezer, 2 Shooting Star, 3 Takuri, 4 Inverted Hammer, 5 Bearish Marubozu, 6 Bearish Tweezer

Quiz 16 Answers	1 Bearish Tweezer, 2 Bullish Tweezer, 3 Bearish Spinning Top, 4 Gravestone, 5 Bearish Tweezer, 6 Dragon Fly

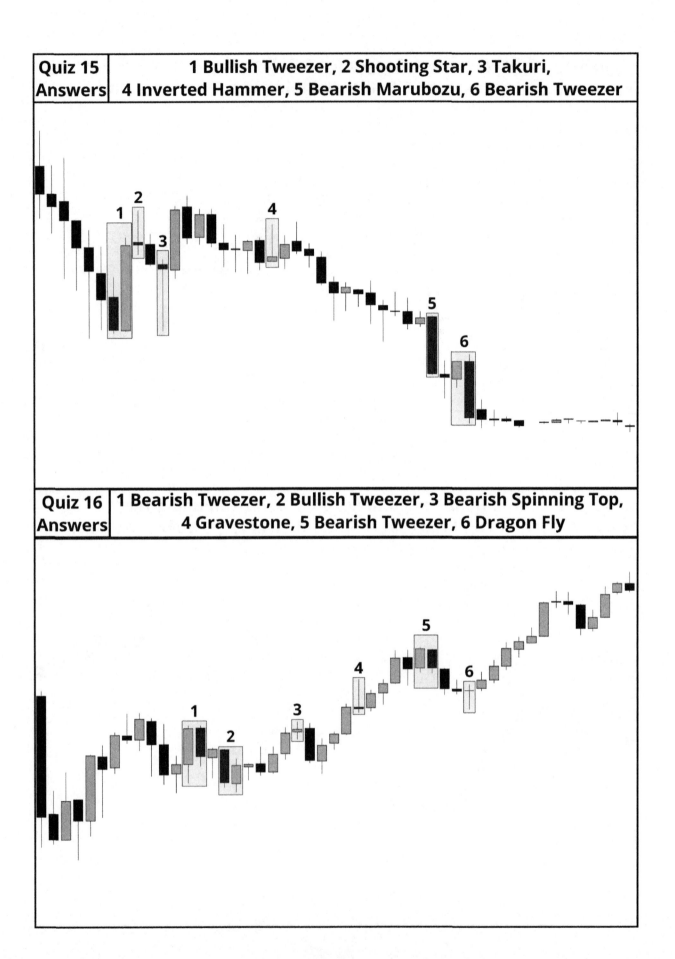

Quiz 17 Answers	1 Three White Soldiers, 2 Bullish Spinning Top, 3 Bearish Tweezer, 4 Bullish Tweezer, 5 Bearish Spinning Top

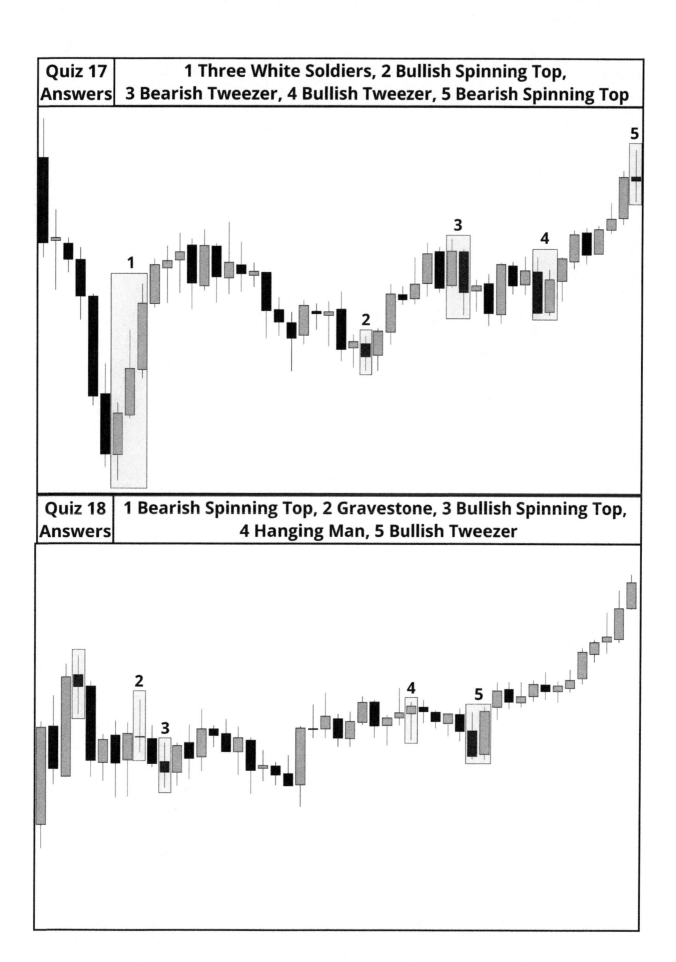

Quiz 18 Answers	1 Bearish Spinning Top, 2 Gravestone, 3 Bullish Spinning Top, 4 Hanging Man, 5 Bullish Tweezer

Quiz 19 Answers	1 Takuri, 2 Hanging Man, 3 Dragonfly, 4 Bearish Tweezer, 5 Bullish Doji, 6 Bearish Rickshaw Man

Quiz 20 Answers	1 Bearish Tweezer, 2 Shooting Star, 3 Hanging Man, 4 Hammer, 5 Three White Soldiers

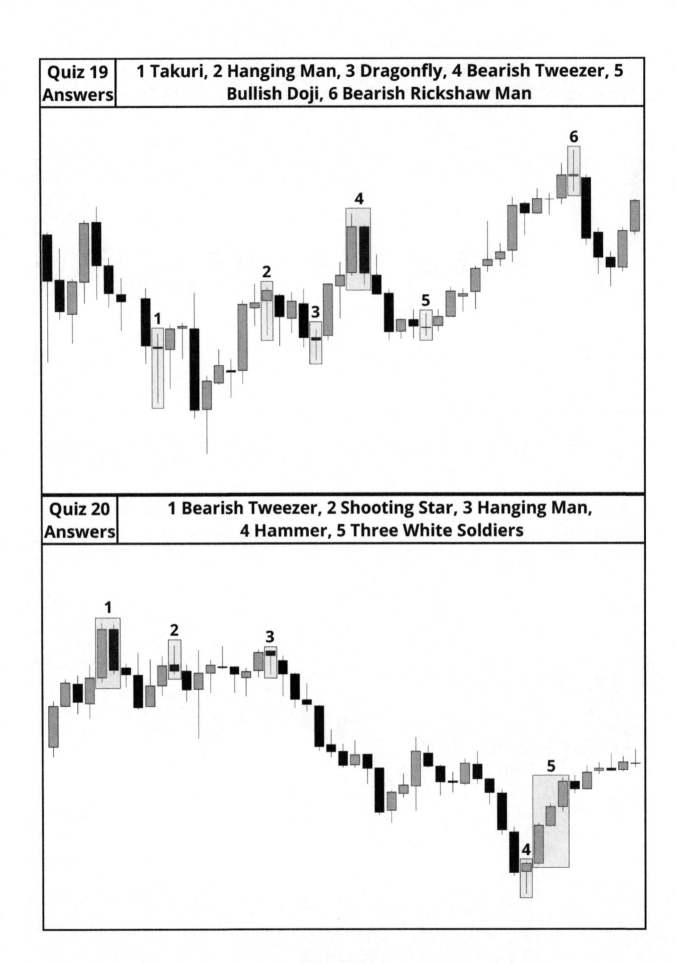

Quiz 21 Answers	1 Three White Soldiers, 2 Bearish Tweezer, 3 Bullish Doji, 4 Bearish Tweezer, 5 Gravestone, 6 Bullish Tweezer

Quiz 22 Answers	1 Bearish Doji, 2 Bullish Spinning Top, 3 Advance Block, 4 Bearish Marubosu, 5 Bullish Tweezer, 6 Bullish Spinning Top

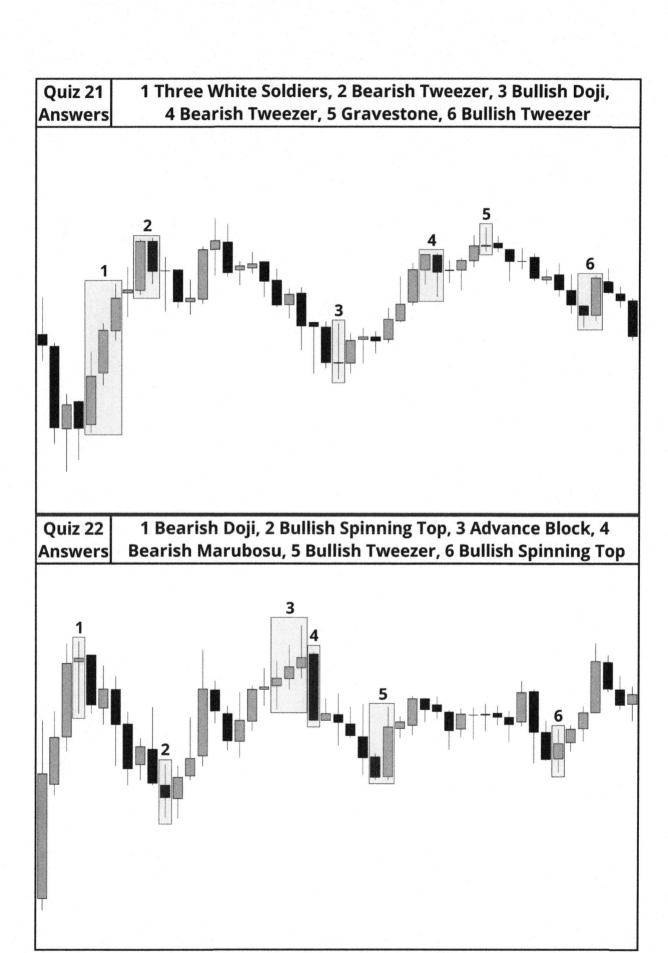

Quiz 23 Answers	1 Bullish Rickshaw Man, 2 Bearish Tweezer, 3 Bullish Tweezer, 4 Flat Top Breakout, 5 Bearish Tweezer, 6 Morning Star

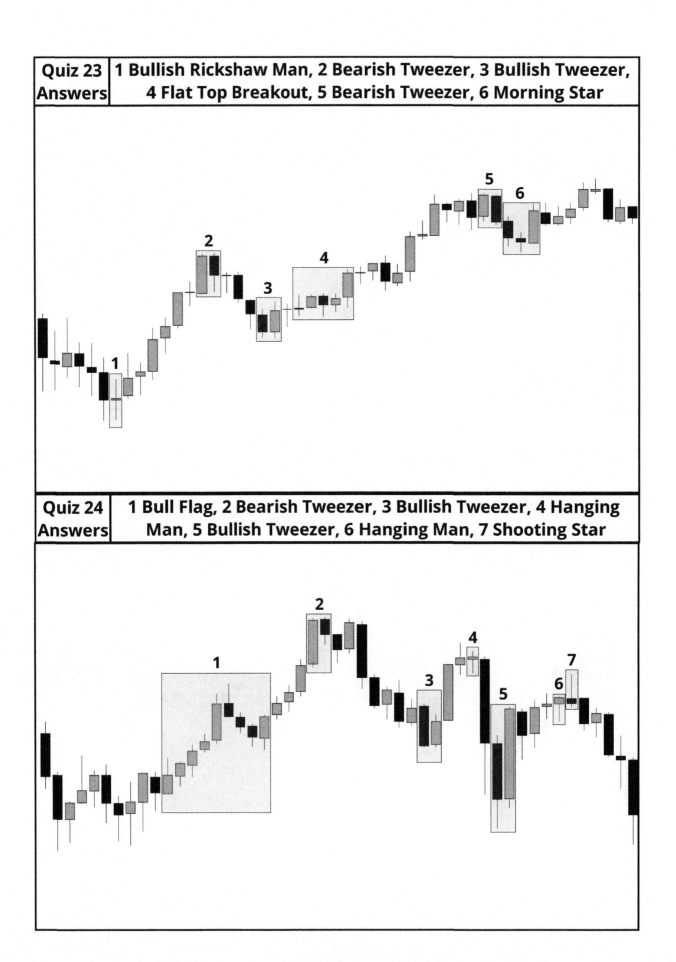

Quiz 24 Answers	1 Bull Flag, 2 Bearish Tweezer, 3 Bullish Tweezer, 4 Hanging Man, 5 Bullish Tweezer, 6 Hanging Man, 7 Shooting Star

Quiz 25 Answers	1 Bullish Spinning Top, 2 Bullish Marubosu, 3 Bearish Doji, 4 Bullish Harami, 5 Flat Top Breakout

Quiz 26 Answers	1 Bullish Spinning Top, 2 Bearish Doji, 3 Bullish Spinning Top, 4 Hammer, 5 Bearish Rickshaw Man, 6 Bullish Marubosu

Quiz 27 Answers	1 Bullish Tweezer, 2 Bullish Doji, 3 Three Black Crows, 4 Takuri, 5 Dragonfly

Quiz 28 Answers	1 Inverted Hammer, 2 Bullish Marubosu, 2 Bearish Tweezer, 4 Bearish Rickshaw Man, 5 Bearish Doji

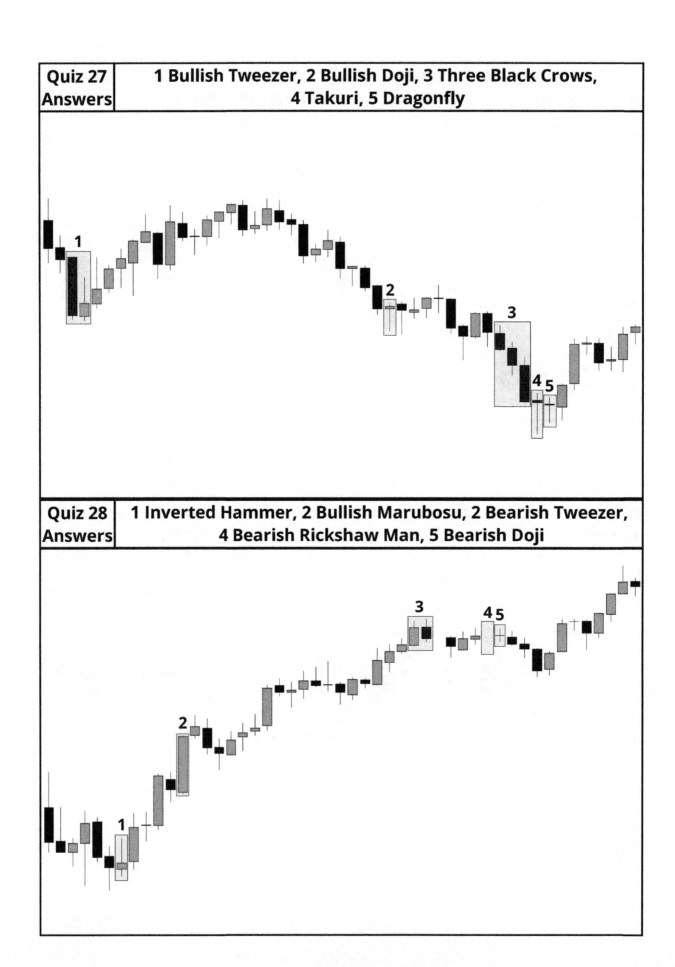

Quiz 29 Answers	1 Hammer, 2 Bearish Tweezer, 3 Bullish Tweezer, 4 Hammer, 5 Hanging Man

Quiz 30 Answers	1 Bullish Marubozu, 2 Bearish Tweezer, 3 Shooting Star, 4 Evening Star, 5 Bearish Doji, 6 Inverted Hammer

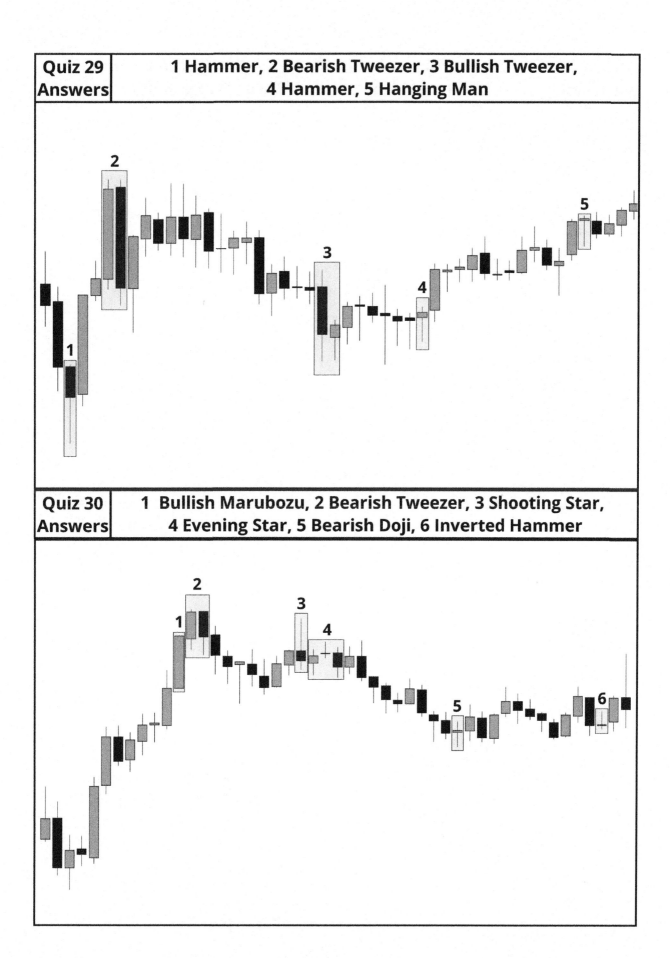

Quiz 31 Answers	1 Hanging Man, 2 Bullish Tweezer, 3 Inverted Hammer, 4 Bullish Spinning Top, 5 Three White Soldiers

Quiz 32 Answers	1 Three Black Crows, 2 Hammer, 3 Bullish Rickshaw Man, 4 Inverted Hammer, 5 Bearish Tweezer, 6 Bullish Doji

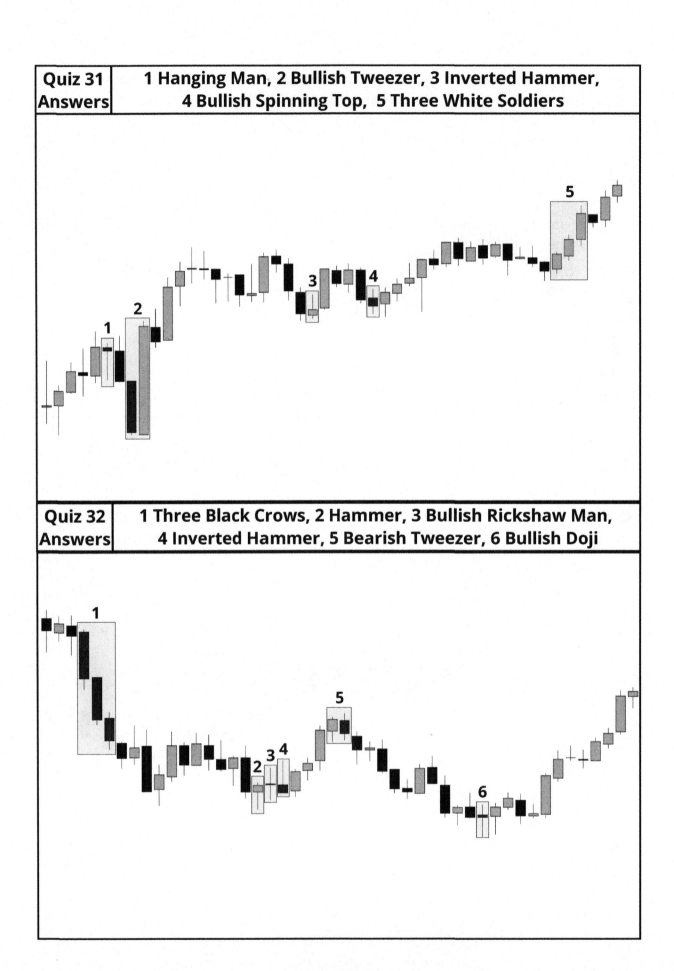

Quiz 33 Answers	1 Bullish Tweezer, 2 Three White Soldiers, 3 Bearish Spinning Top, 4 Dragonfly, 5 Bear Flag

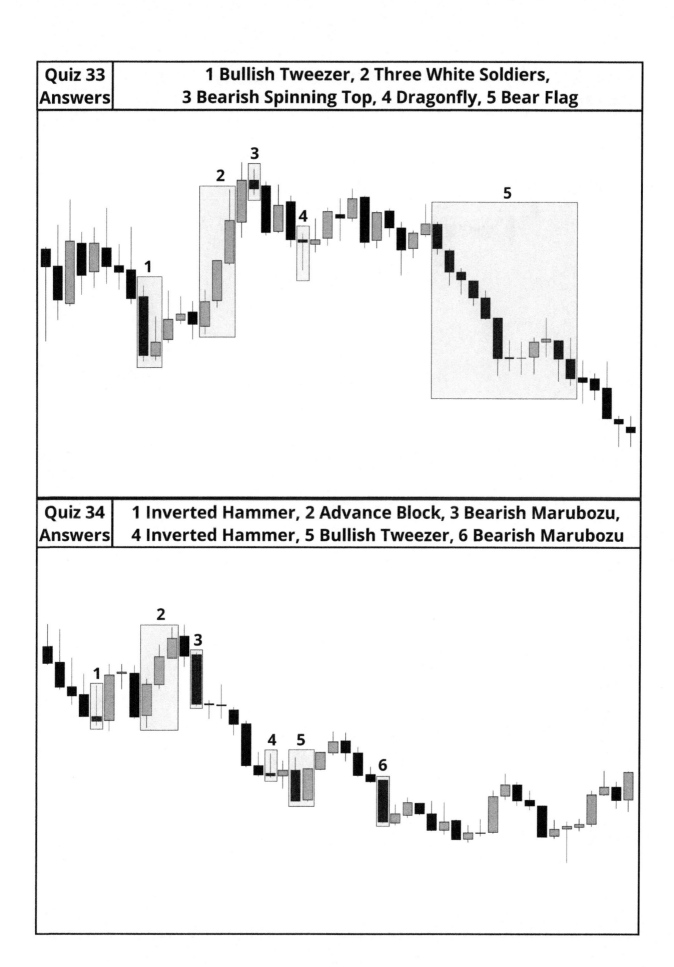

Quiz 34 Answers	1 Inverted Hammer, 2 Advance Block, 3 Bearish Marubozu, 4 Inverted Hammer, 5 Bullish Tweezer, 6 Bearish Marubozu

Quiz 35 Answers	1 Bearish Tweezer, 2 Bullish Spinning Top, 3 Bearish Rickshaw Man, 4 Advance Block, 5 Bullish Tweezer

Quiz 36 Answers	1 Bearish Spinning Top, 2 Bearish Tweezer, 3 Three Black Crows, 4 Dragonfly, 5 Three White Soldiers

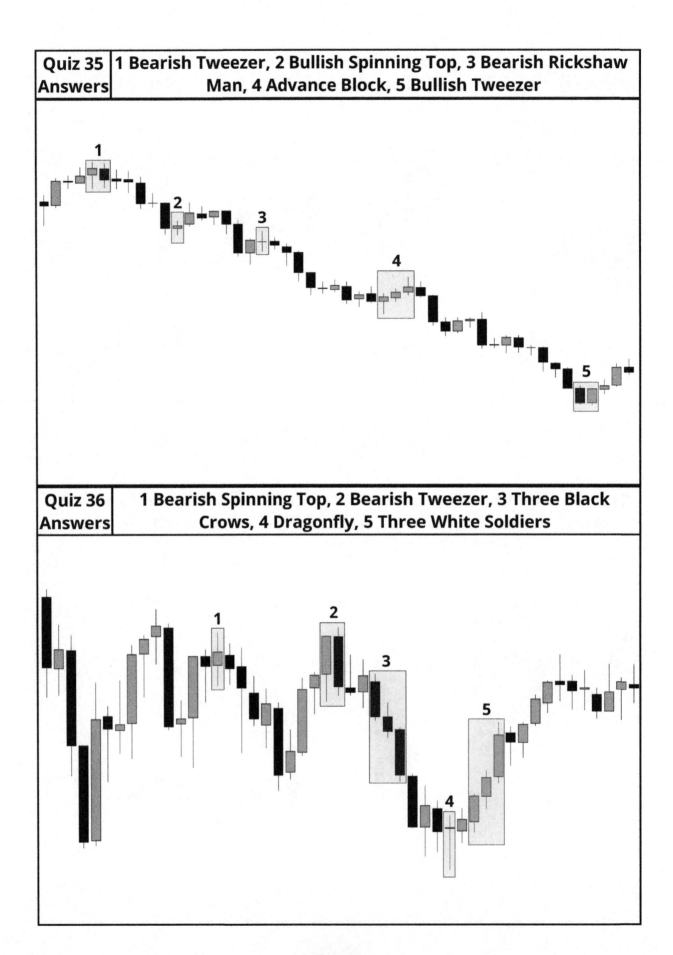

Quiz 37 Answers	1 Bullish Tweezer, 2 Bearish Tweezer, 3 Bullish Spinning Top, 4 Shooting Star, 5 Bearish Doji

Quiz 38 Answers	1 Inverted Hammer, 2 Hammer, 3 Bearish Tweezer, 4 Bullish Tweezer, 5 Bearish Spinning Top, 6 Bearish Tweezer

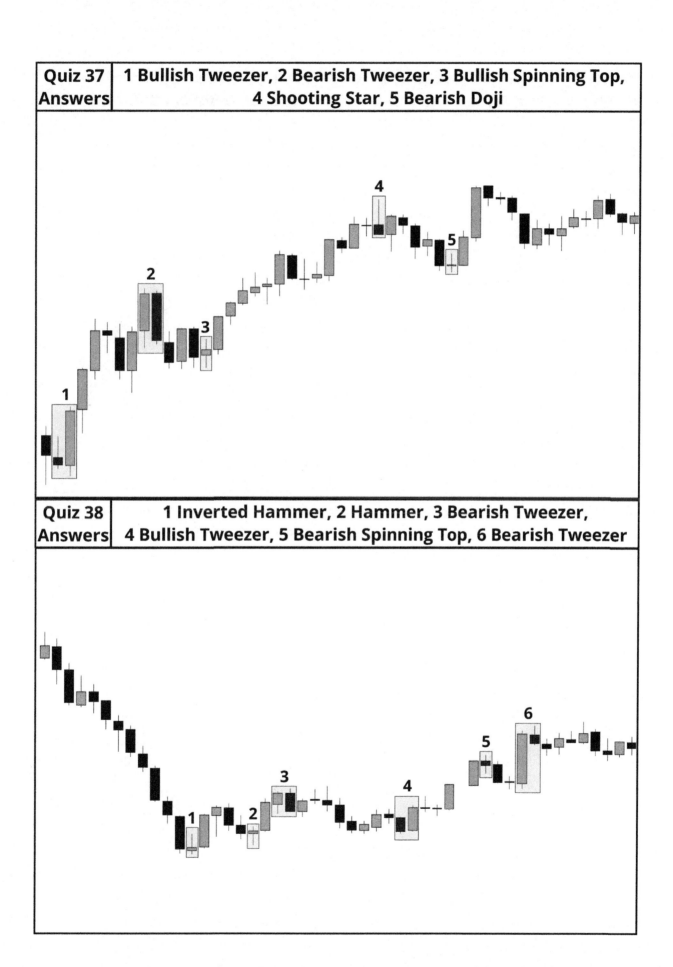

Quiz 39 Answers	1 Bearish Tweezer, 2 Hanging Man, 3 Bullish Spinning Top, 4 Engulfing Candle, 5 Bearish Tweezer, 6 Bullish Spinning Top

Quiz 40 Answers	1 Bullish Tweezer, 2 Hammer, 3 Inverted Hammer, 4 Shooting Star, 5 Bearish Tweezer

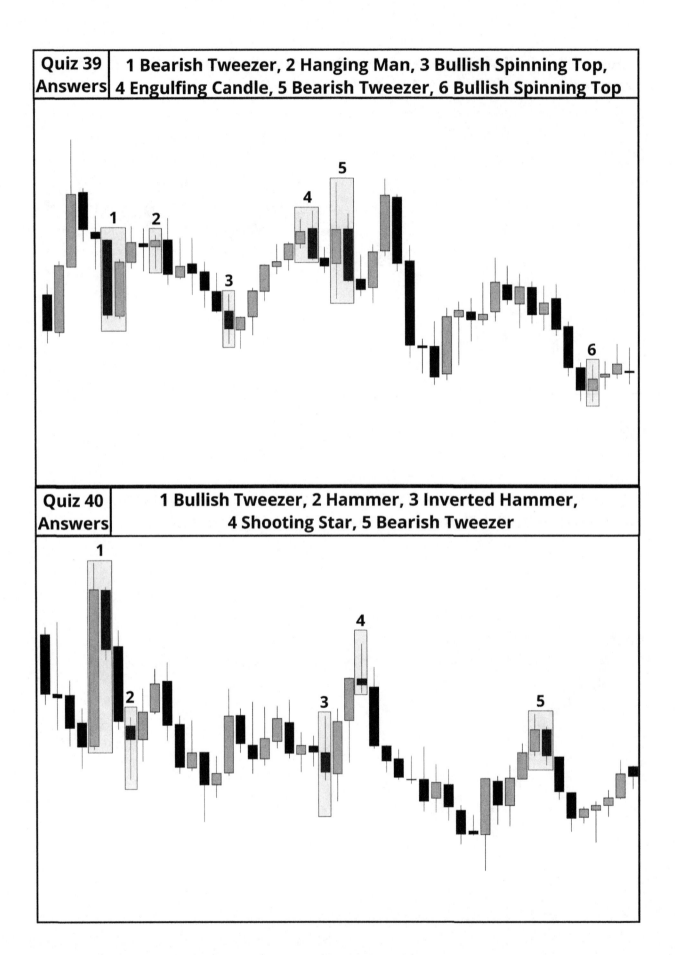

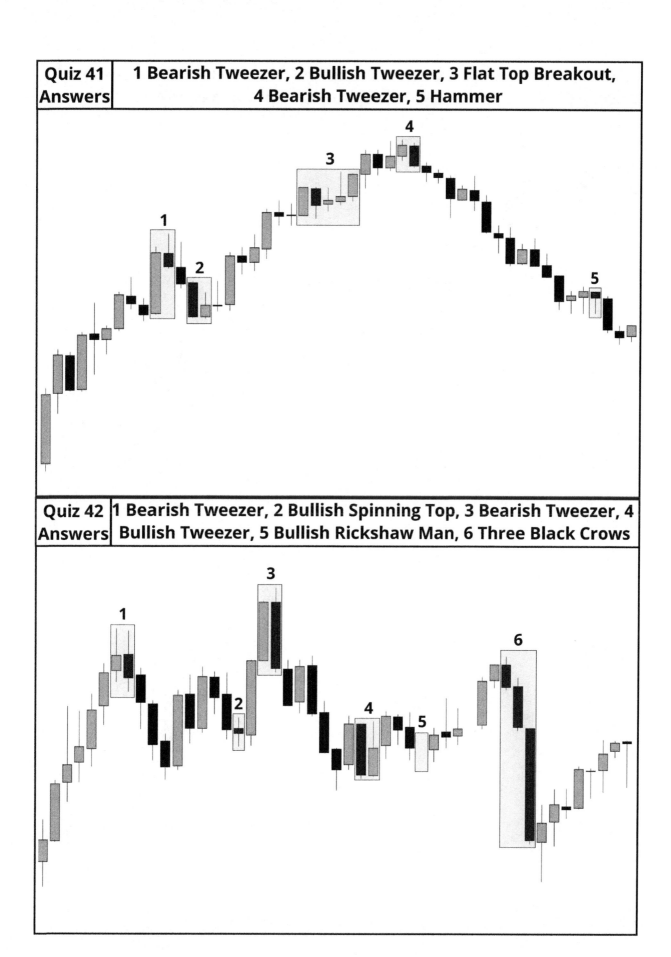

Quiz 41 Answers	1 Bearish Tweezer, 2 Bullish Tweezer, 3 Flat Top Breakout, 4 Bearish Tweezer, 5 Hammer

Quiz 42 Answers	1 Bearish Tweezer, 2 Bullish Spinning Top, 3 Bearish Tweezer, 4 Bullish Tweezer, 5 Bullish Rickshaw Man, 6 Three Black Crows

Quiz 43 Answers	1 Inverted Hammer, 2 Bullish Tweezer, 3 Bullish Tweezer, 4 Bearish Spinning Top, 5 Dragonfly

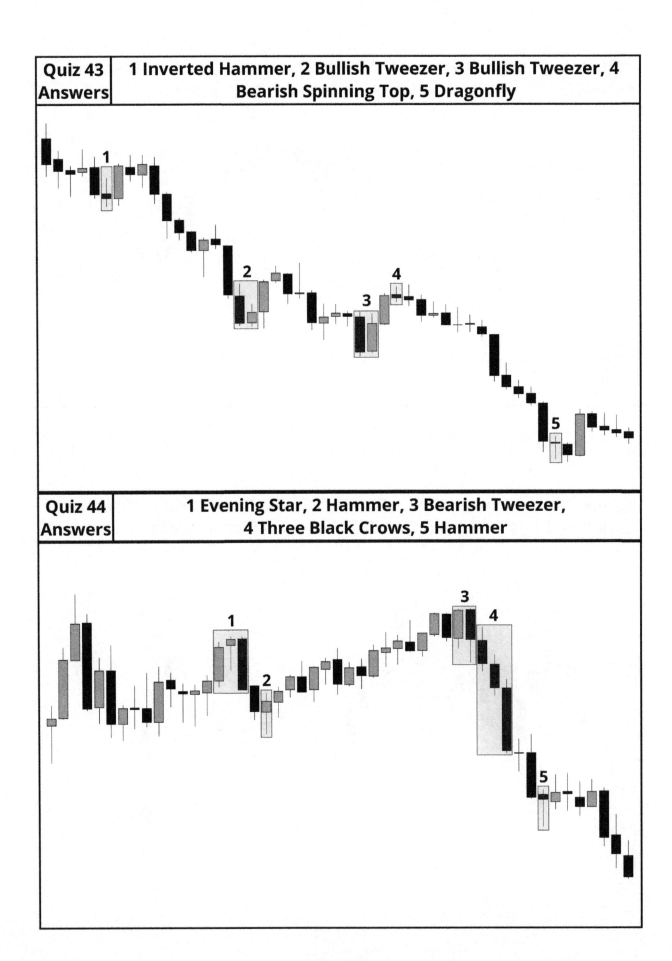

Quiz 44 Answers	1 Evening Star, 2 Hammer, 3 Bearish Tweezer, 4 Three Black Crows, 5 Hammer

Quiz 45 Answers	1 Bearish Tweezer, 2 Bearish Spinning Top, 4 Dragonfly, 5 Bullish Tweezer, 6 Gravestone, 7 Hammer

Quiz 46 Answers	1 Bullish Rickshaw Man, 2 Bearish Rickshaw Man, 3 Bullish Doji, 4 Bear Flag, 5 Three White Soldiers

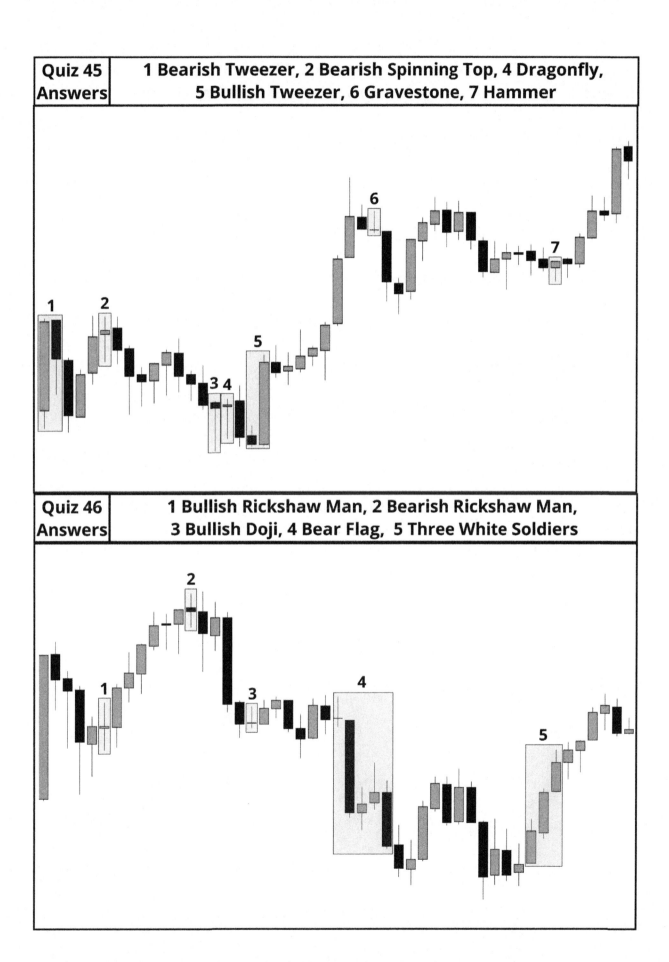

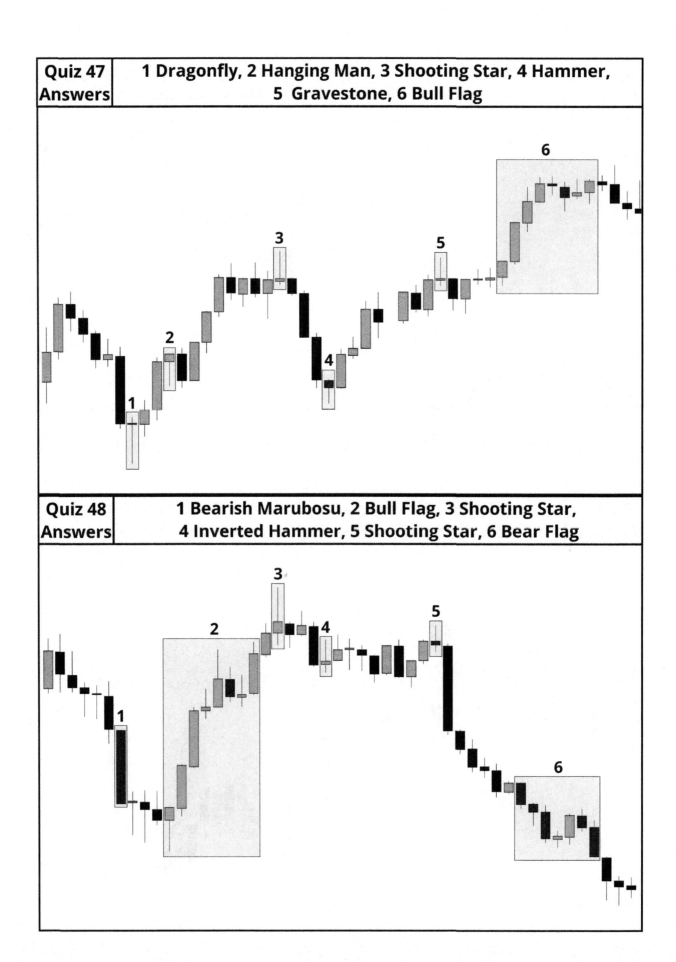

Quiz 47 Answers	1 Dragonfly, 2 Hanging Man, 3 Shooting Star, 4 Hammer, 5 Gravestone, 6 Bull Flag

| Quiz 48 Answers | 1 Bearish Marubosu, 2 Bull Flag, 3 Shooting Star, 4 Inverted Hammer, 5 Shooting Star, 6 Bear Flag |

Quiz 49 Answers	1 Hammer, 2 Three Black Crows, 3 Bearish Tweezer, 4 Shooting Star, 5 Inverted Hammer

Quiz 50 Answers	1 Hanging Man, 2 Bullish Tweezer, 3 Three Black Crows, 4 Bearish Marubosu, 5 Hammer, 6 Bullish Tweezer

Chapter 4

Advanced Challenge

Find and Name the

Candlestick Patterns

Find and Name the Candlestick Patterns

Welcome to the Advanced Challenge. In the following charts a number of patterns have been found. We will not reveal which patterns to find, just how many there are. Mark or note the patterns you identify. Feel free to repeat the challenge to improve your score.

| Quiz Number | The minimum number of candlestick patterns to be found in this chart |

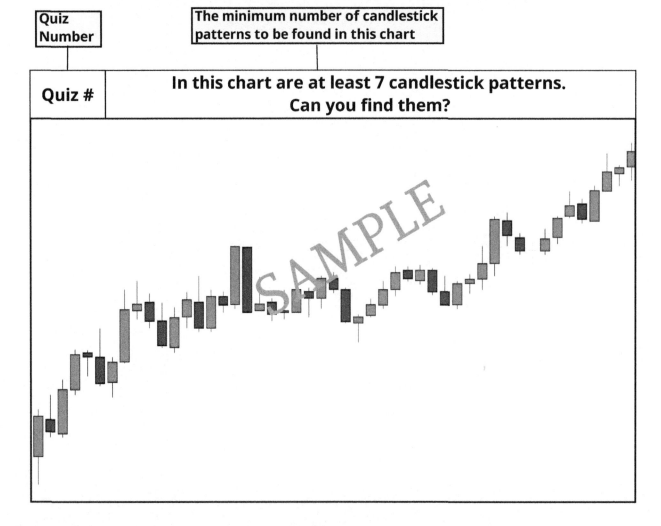

| Quiz # | In this chart are at least 7 candlestick patterns. Can you find them? |

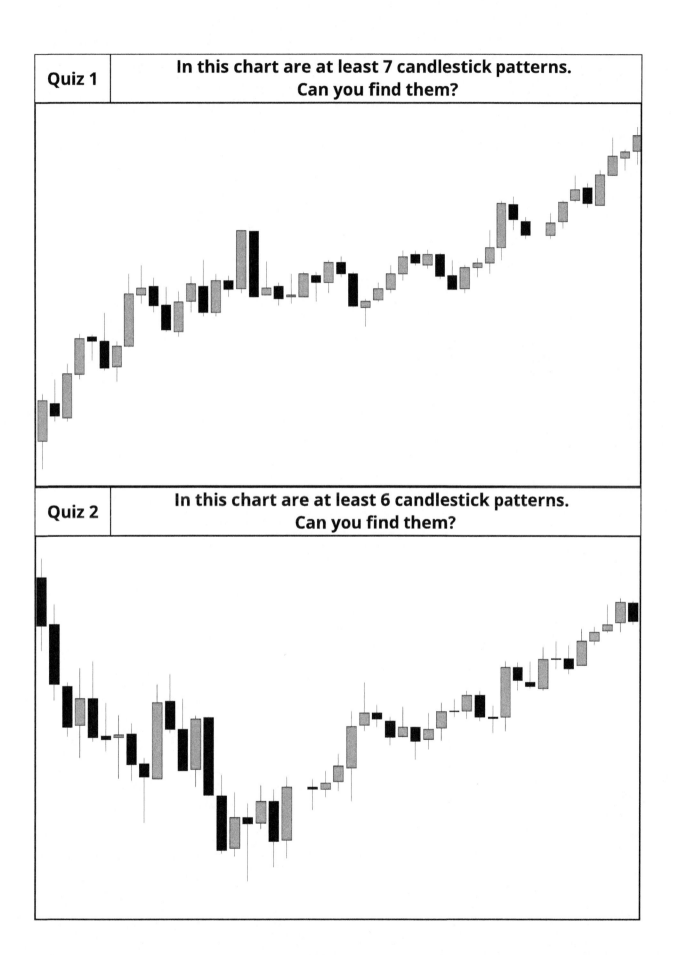

| Quiz 1 | **In this chart are at least 7 candlestick patterns.**
 Can you find them? |

| Quiz 2 | **In this chart are at least 6 candlestick patterns.**
 Can you find them? |

Quiz 3	**In this chart are at least 6 candlestick patterns.** **Can you find them?**

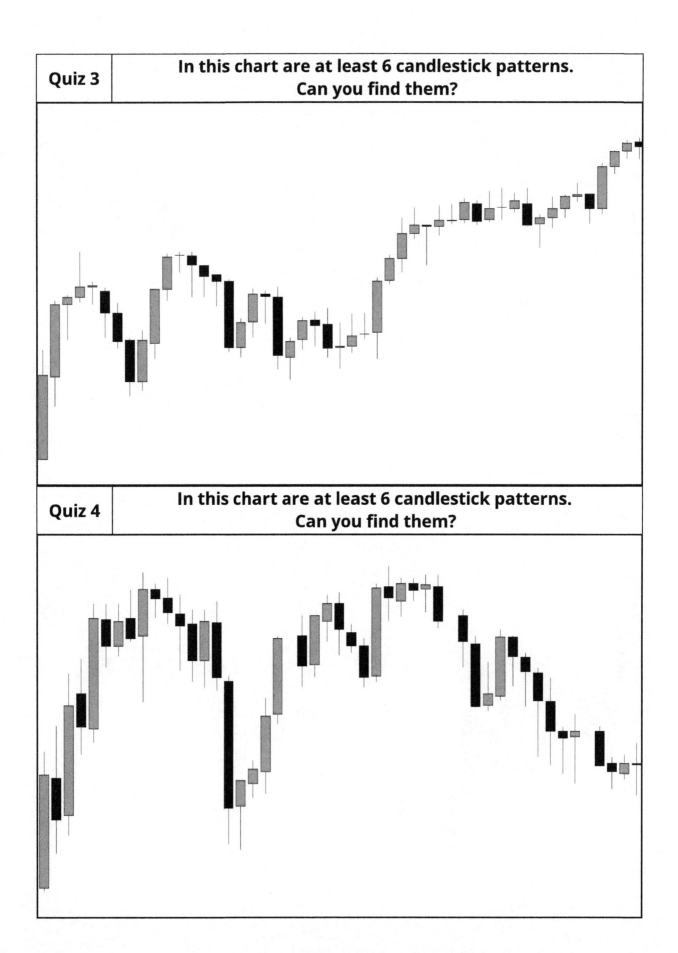

Quiz 4	**In this chart are at least 6 candlestick patterns.** **Can you find them?**

Quiz 5	**In this chart are at least 7 candlestick patterns.** **Can you find them?**

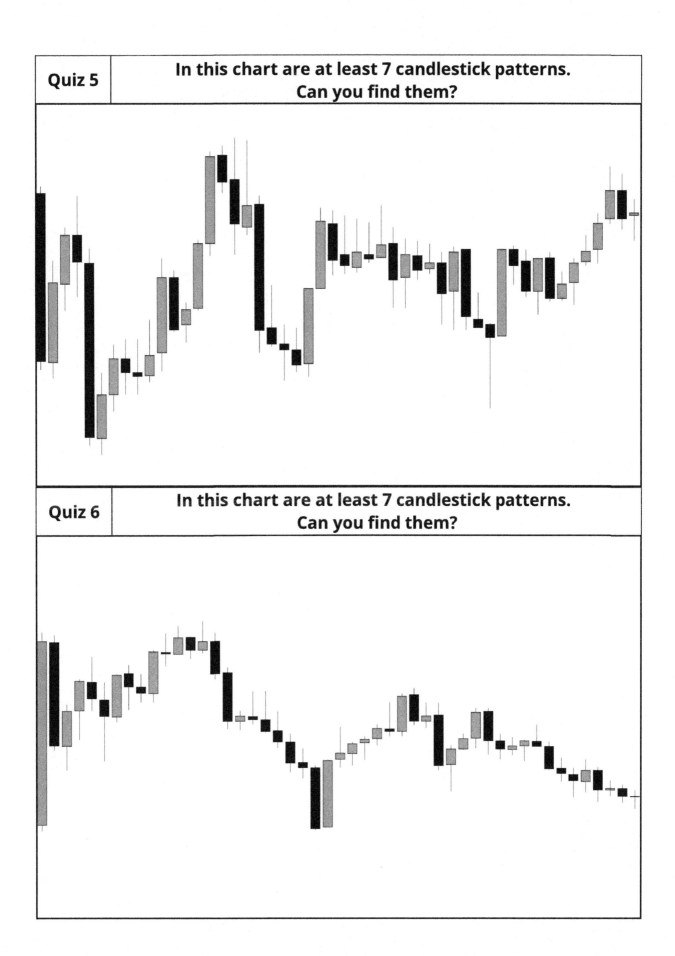

Quiz 6	**In this chart are at least 7 candlestick patterns.** **Can you find them?**

Quiz 7 Answers	In this chart are at least 6 candlestick patterns. Can you find them?

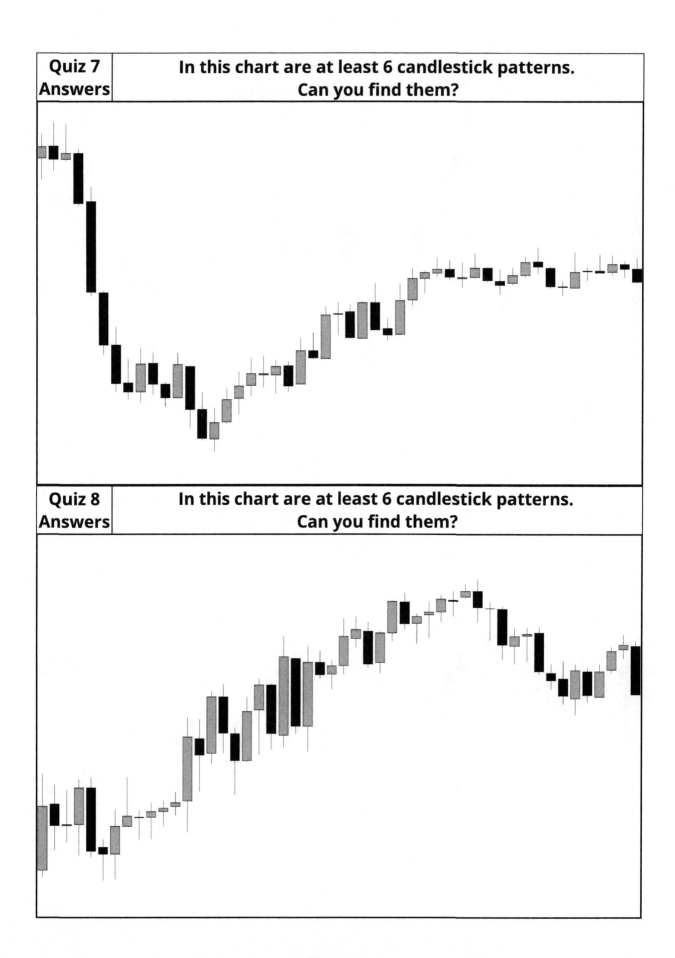

Quiz 8 Answers	In this chart are at least 6 candlestick patterns. Can you find them?

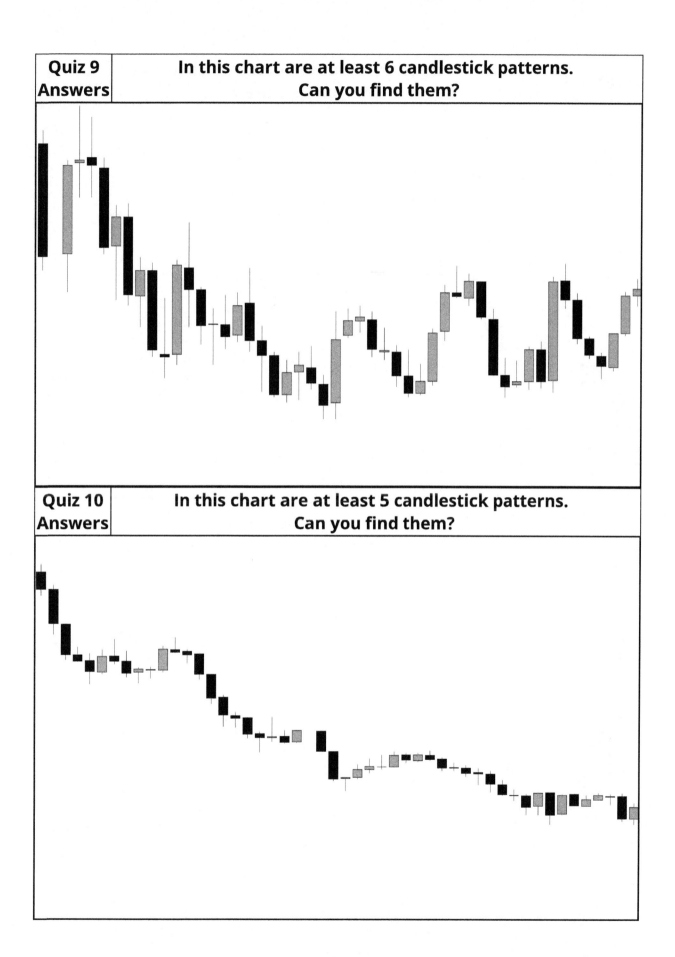

Quiz 11	**In this chart are at least 5 candlestick patterns.** **Can you find them?**

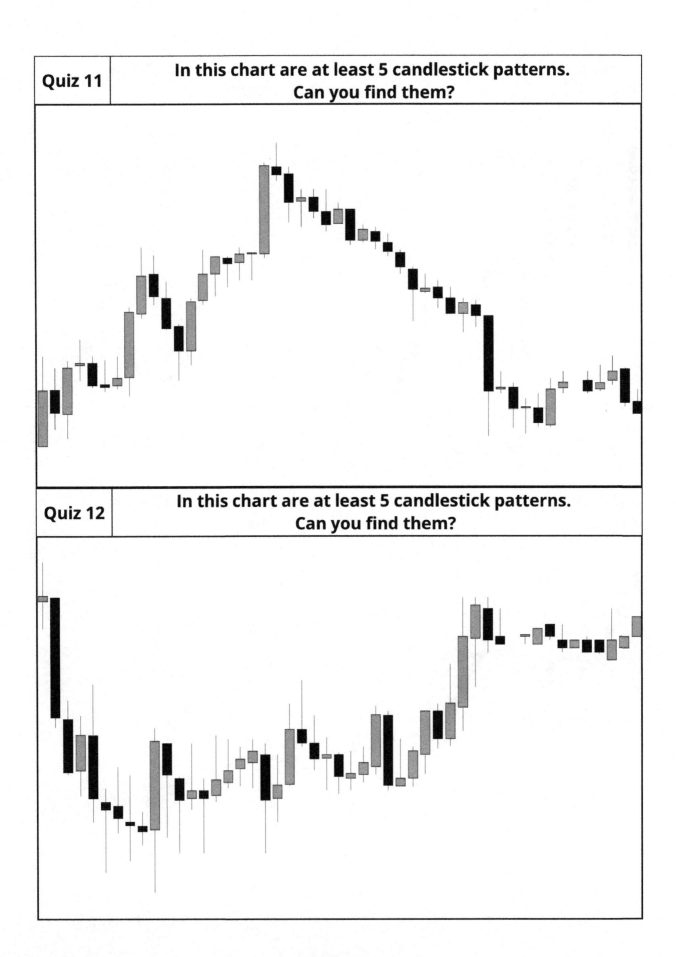

Quiz 12	**In this chart are at least 5 candlestick patterns.** **Can you find them?**

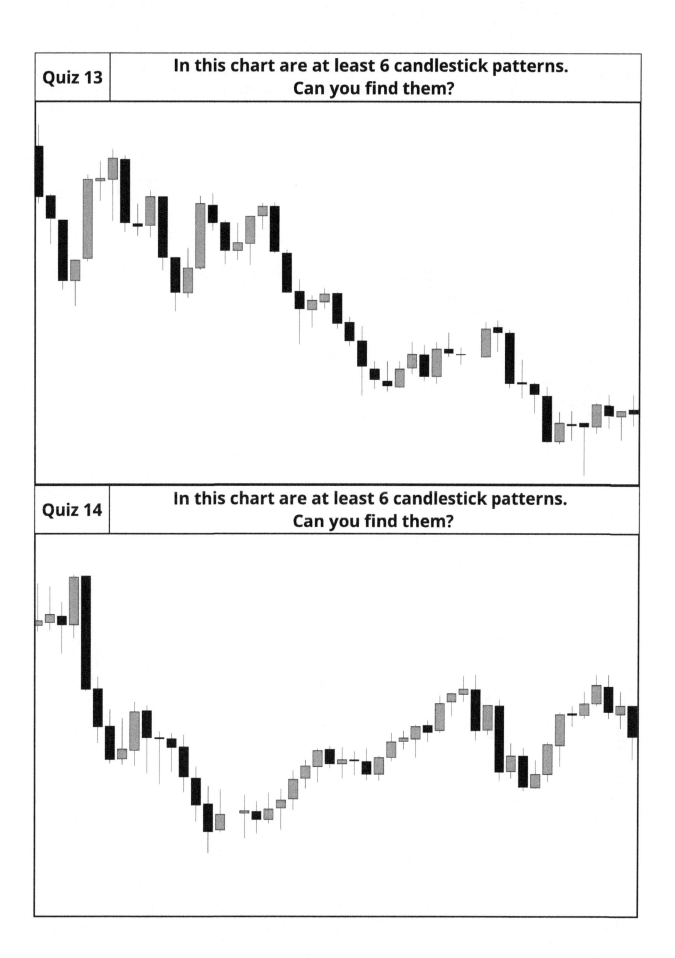

Quiz 13	**In this chart are at least 6 candlestick patterns.** **Can you find them?**

Quiz 14	**In this chart are at least 6 candlestick patterns.** **Can you find them?**

Quiz 15	**In this chart are at least 5 candlestick patterns.** **Can you find them?**

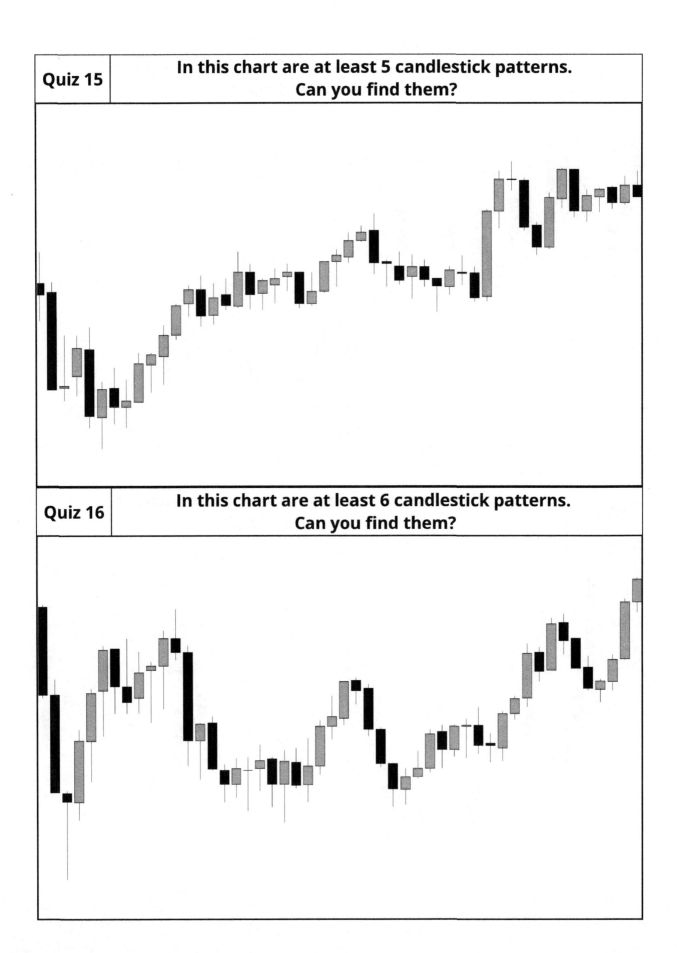

Quiz 16	**In this chart are at least 6 candlestick patterns.** **Can you find them?**

Quiz 17	In this chart are at least 5 candlestick patterns. Can you find them?

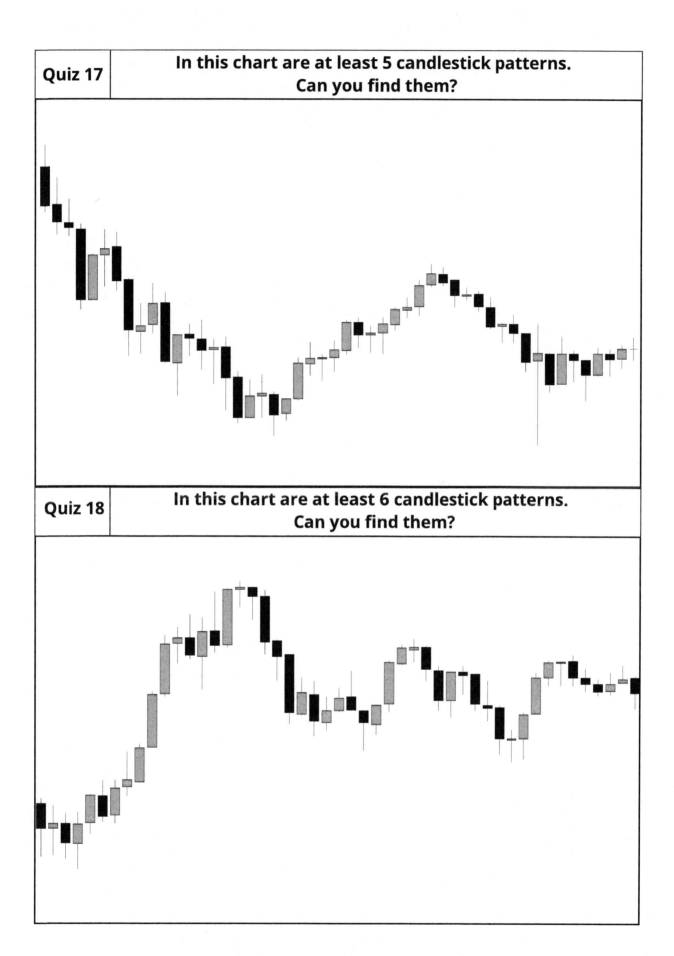

Quiz 18	In this chart are at least 6 candlestick patterns. Can you find them?

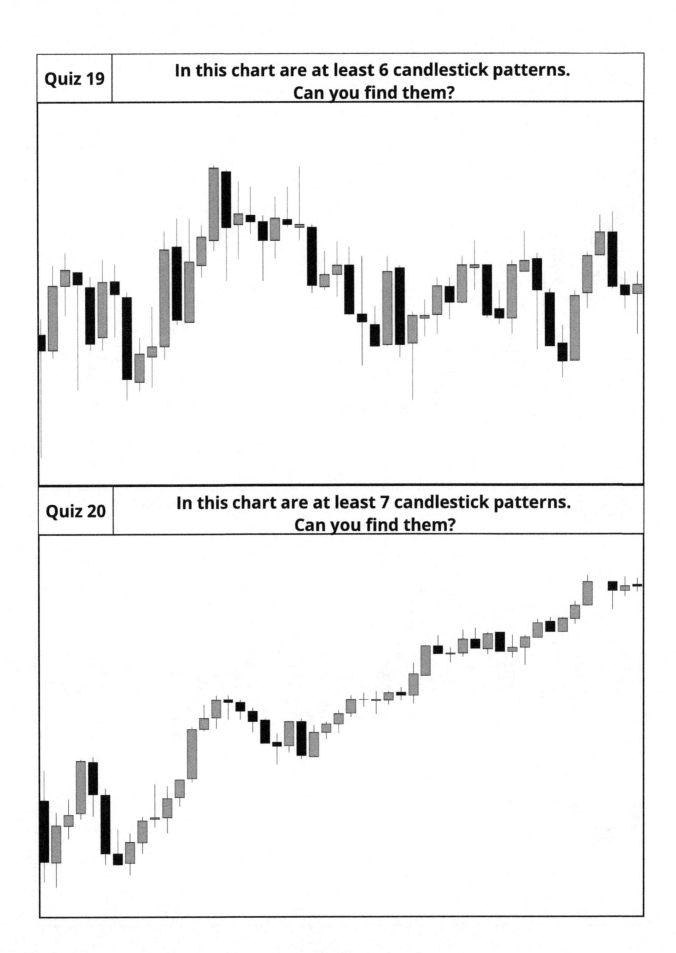

Quiz 19 — In this chart are at least 6 candlestick patterns. Can you find them?

Quiz 20 — In this chart are at least 7 candlestick patterns. Can you find them?

	In this chart are at least 5 candlestick patterns.
Quiz 21	Can you find them?

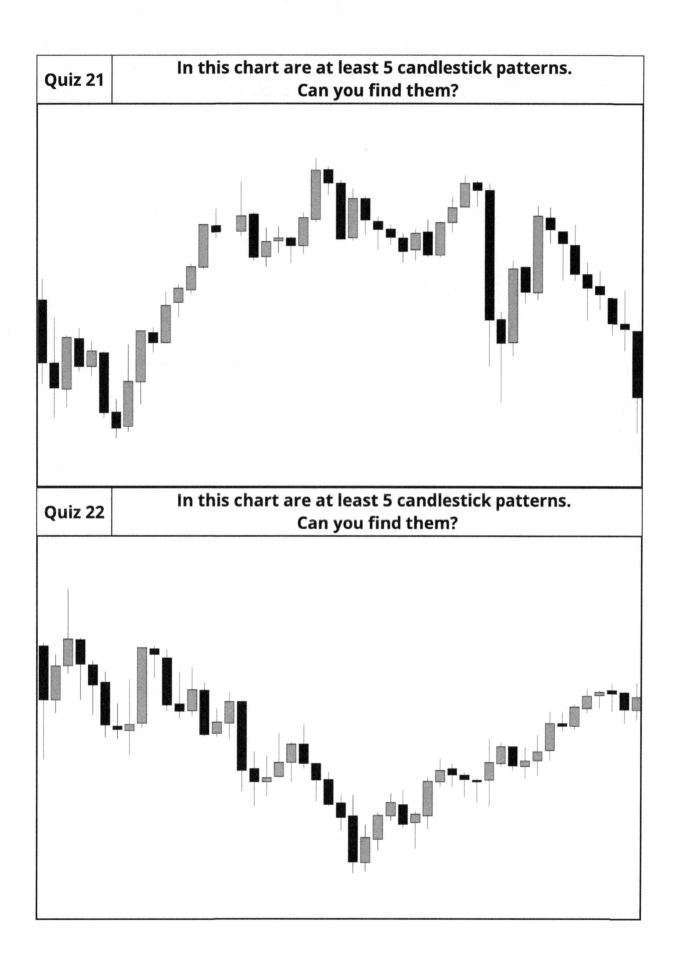

	In this chart are at least 5 candlestick patterns.
Quiz 22	Can you find them?

Quiz 23	In this chart are at least 4 candlestick patterns. Can you find them?

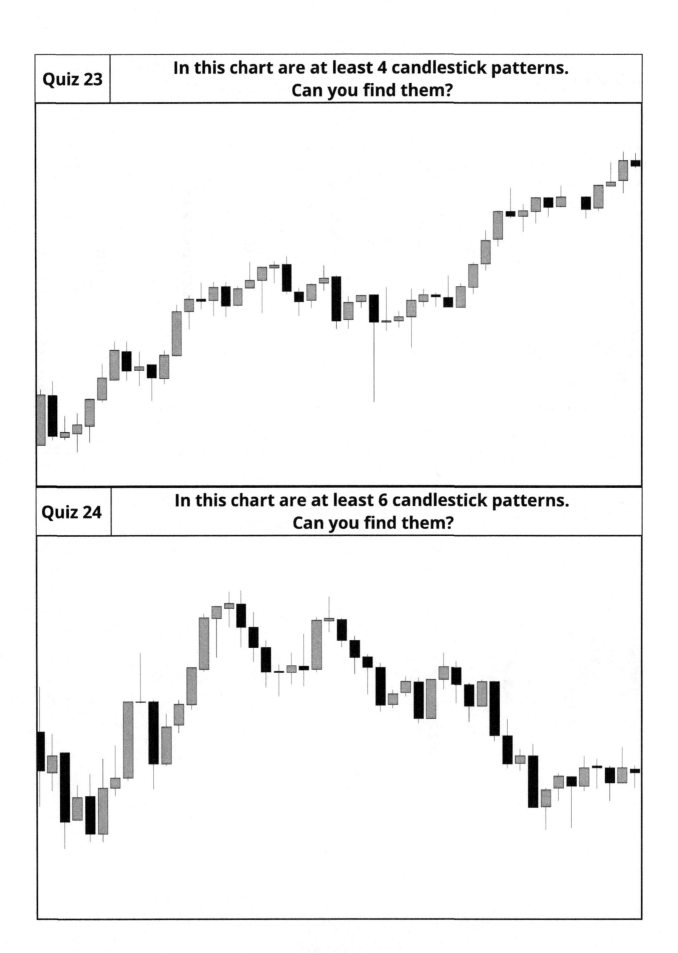

Quiz 24	In this chart are at least 6 candlestick patterns. Can you find them?

Quiz 25	**In this chart are at least 6 candlestick patterns.** **Can you find them?**

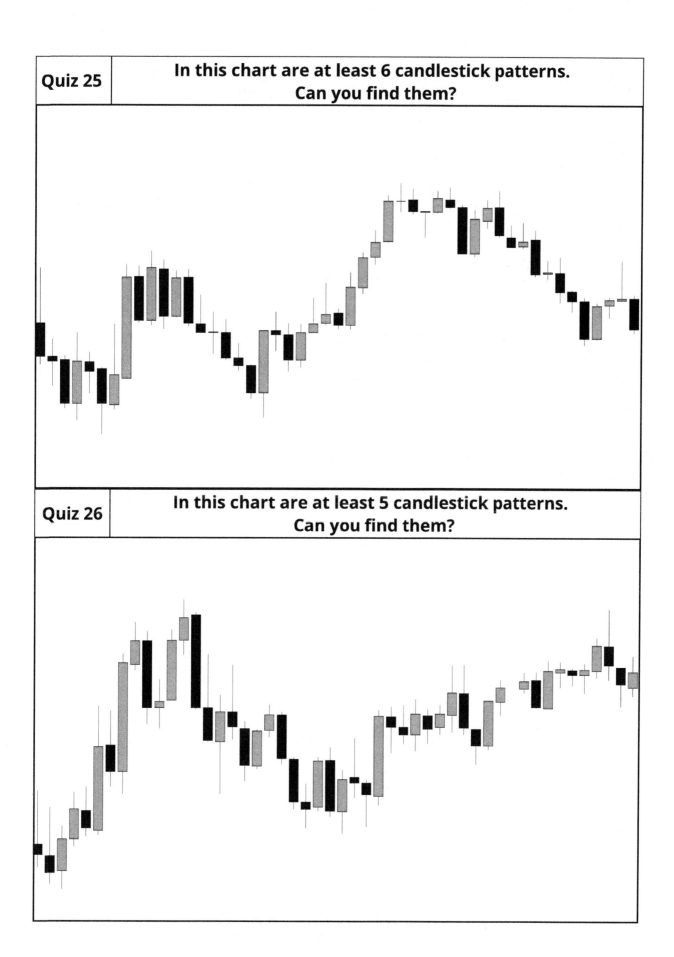

Quiz 26	**In this chart are at least 5 candlestick patterns.** **Can you find them?**

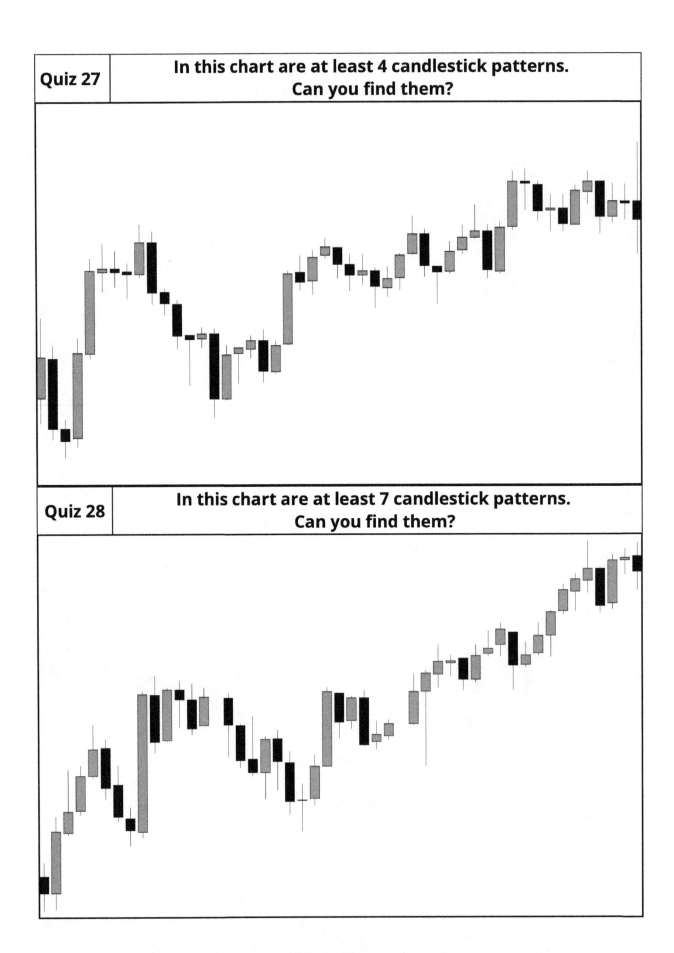

Quiz 27	**In this chart are at least 4 candlestick patterns. Can you find them?**

Quiz 28	**In this chart are at least 7 candlestick patterns. Can you find them?**

Quiz 29	**In this chart are at least 5 candlestick patterns.** **Can you find them?**

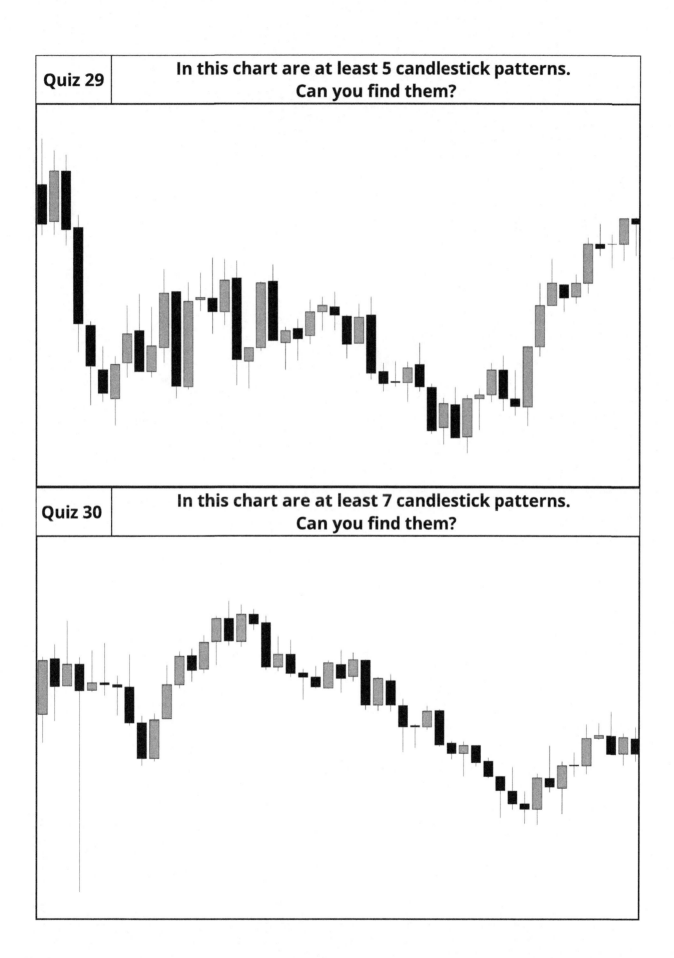

Quiz 30	**In this chart are at least 7 candlestick patterns.** **Can you find them?**

Quiz 31	**In this chart are at least 6 candlestick patterns.** **Can you find them?**

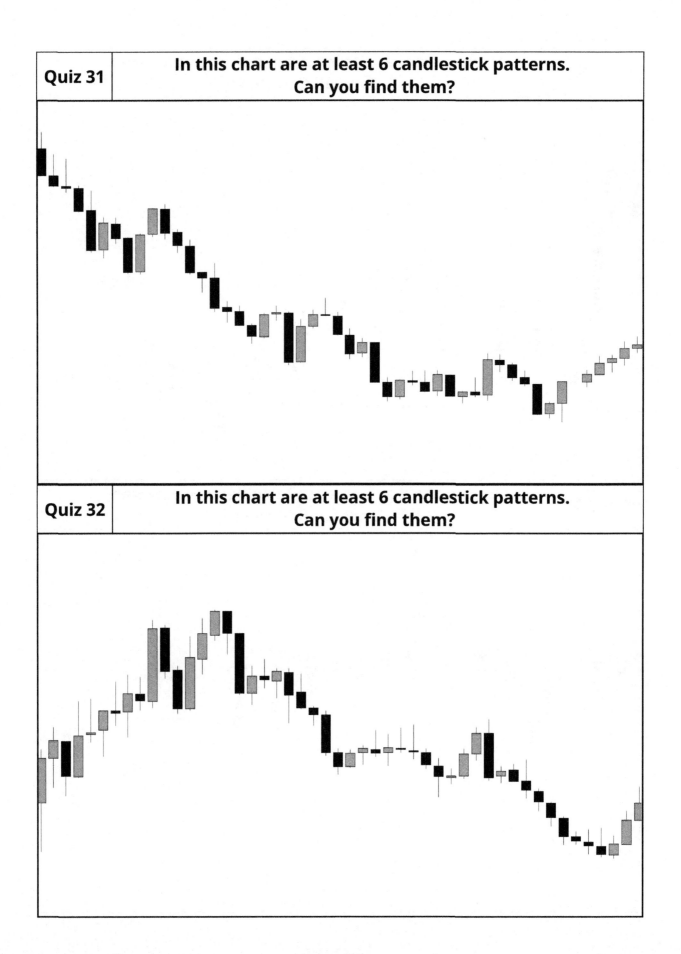

Quiz 32	**In this chart are at least 6 candlestick patterns.** **Can you find them?**

Quiz 33	In this chart are at least 6 candlestick patterns. Can you find them?

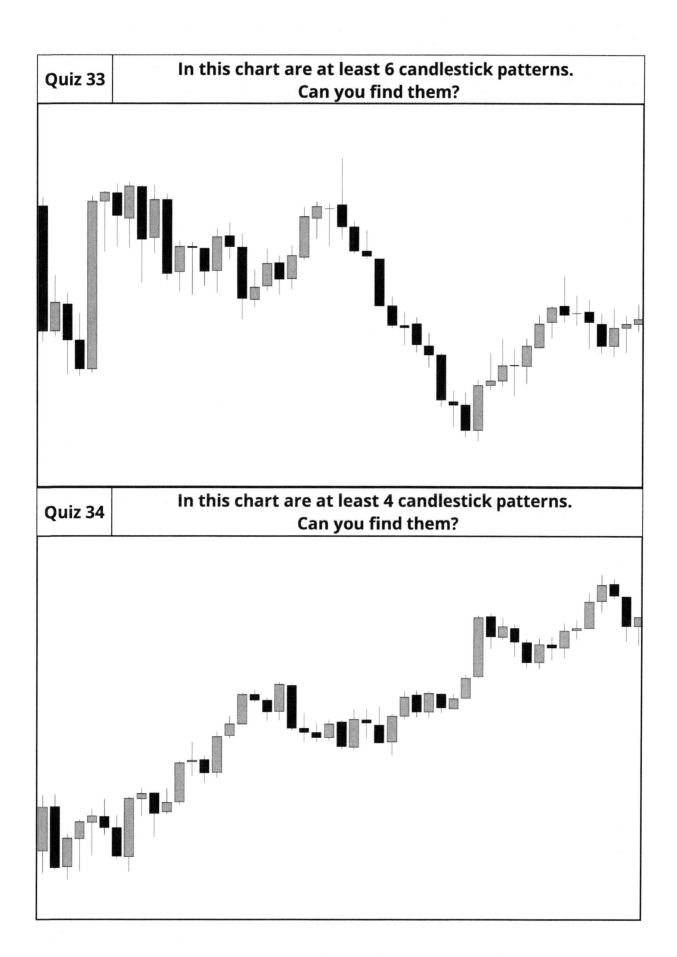

Quiz 34	In this chart are at least 4 candlestick patterns. Can you find them?

Quiz 35	In this chart are at least 6 candlestick patterns. Can you find them?

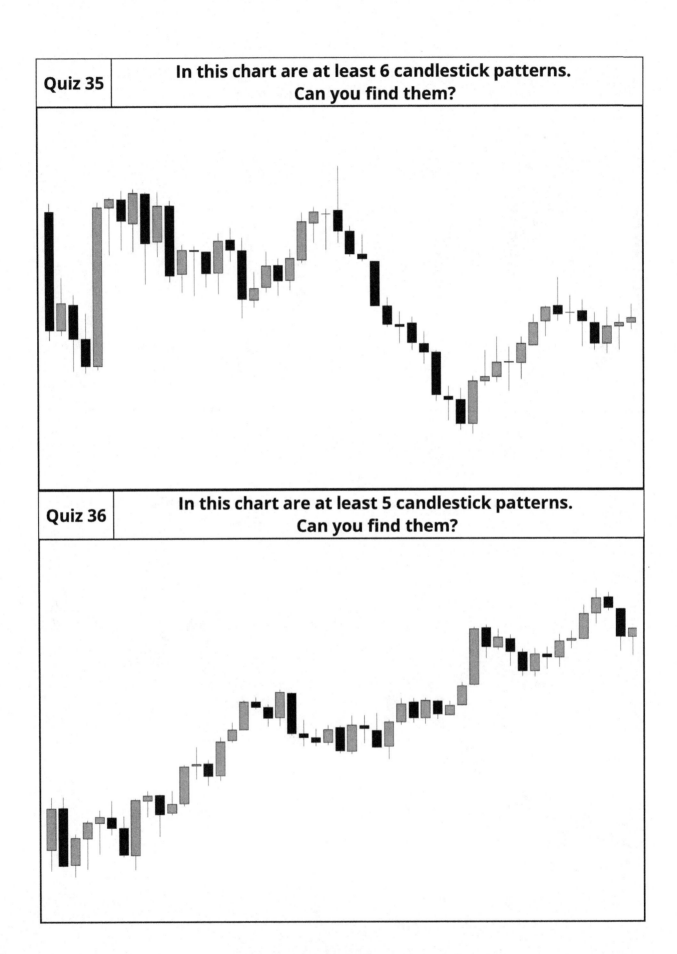

Quiz 36	In this chart are at least 5 candlestick patterns. Can you find them?

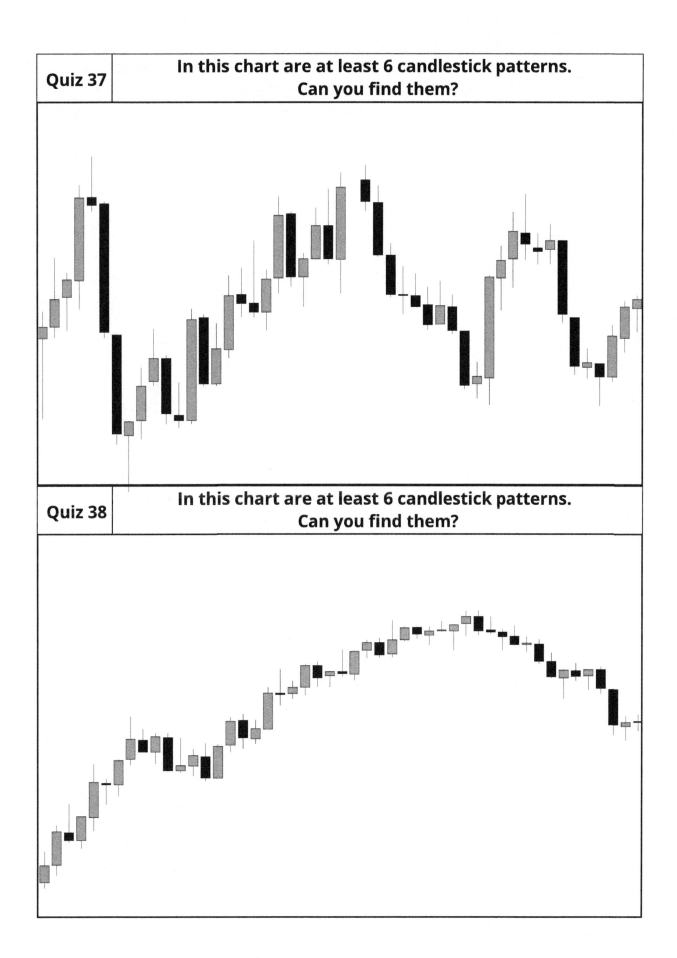

| Quiz 37 | **In this chart are at least 6 candlestick patterns.
Can you find them?** |

| Quiz 38 | **In this chart are at least 6 candlestick patterns.
Can you find them?** |

Quiz 39	**In this chart are at least 6 candlestick patterns. Can you find them?**

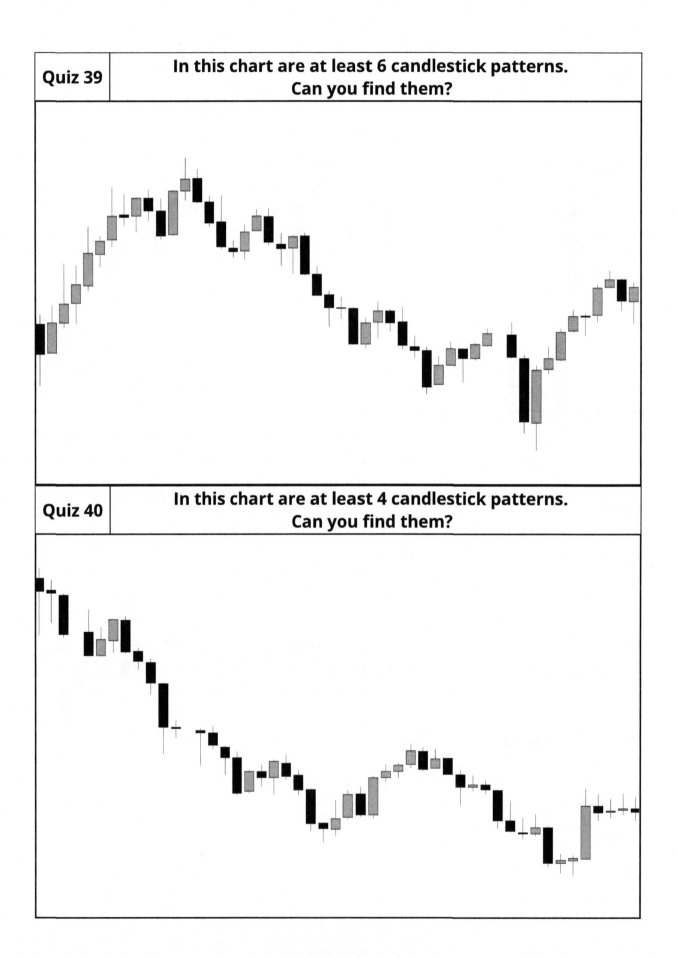

Quiz 40	**In this chart are at least 4 candlestick patterns. Can you find them?**

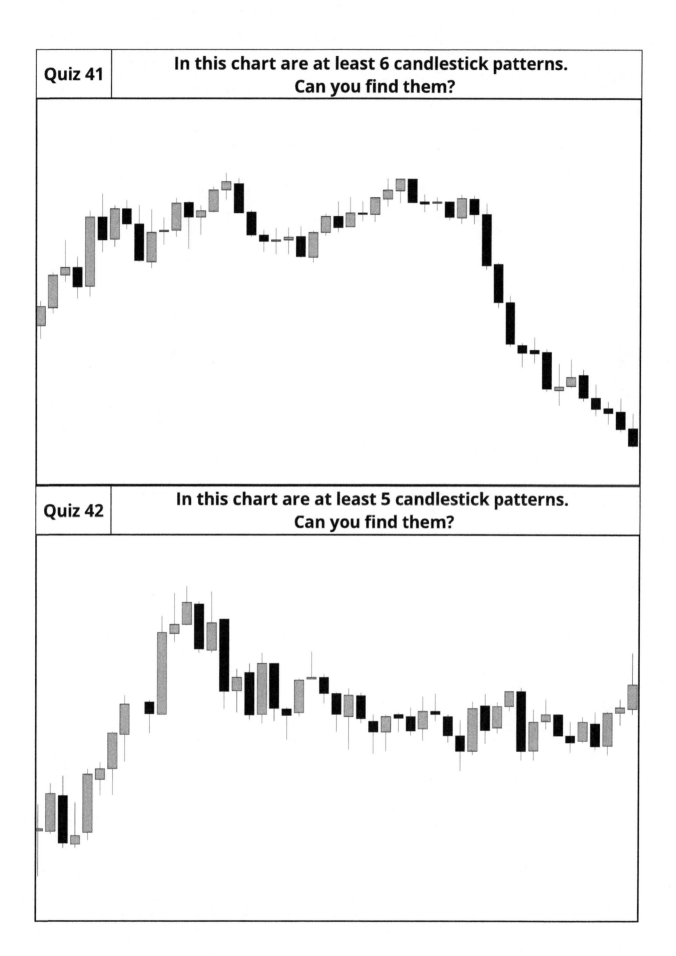

Quiz 43	**In this chart are at least 5 candlestick patterns.** **Can you find them?**

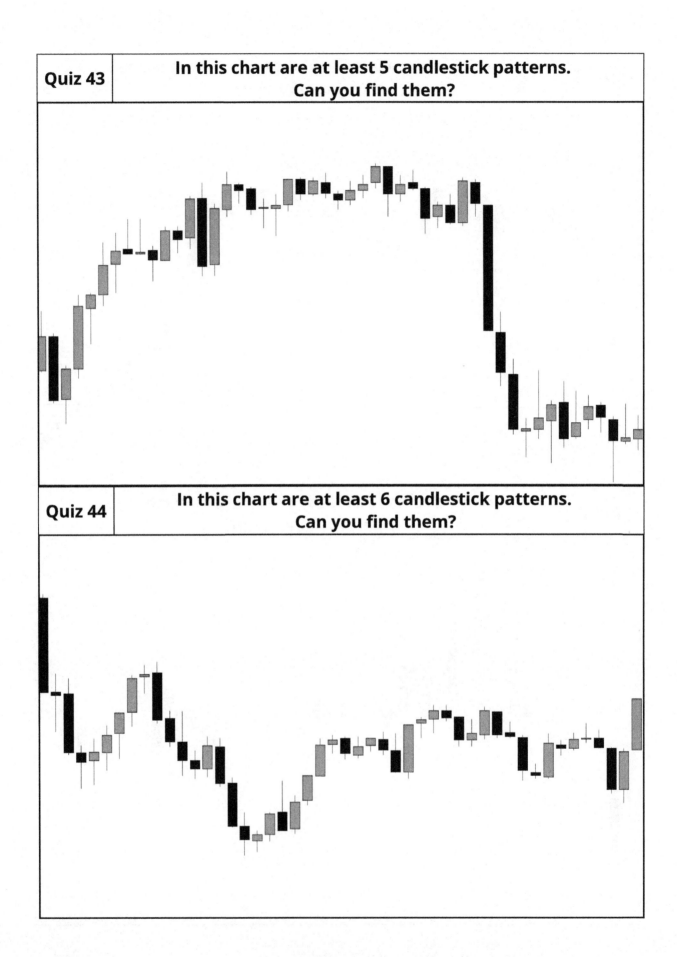

Quiz 44	**In this chart are at least 6 candlestick patterns.** **Can you find them?**

Quiz 45	**In this chart are at least 6 candlestick patterns.** **Can you find them?**

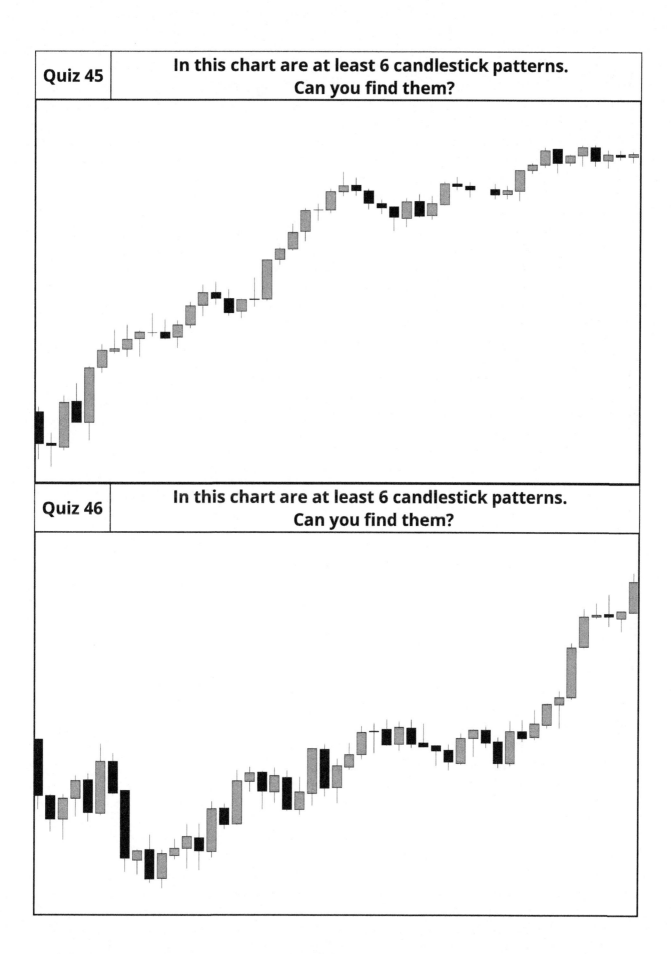

Quiz 46	**In this chart are at least 6 candlestick patterns.** **Can you find them?**

Quiz 47	**In this chart are at least 6 candlestick patterns.** **Can you find them?**

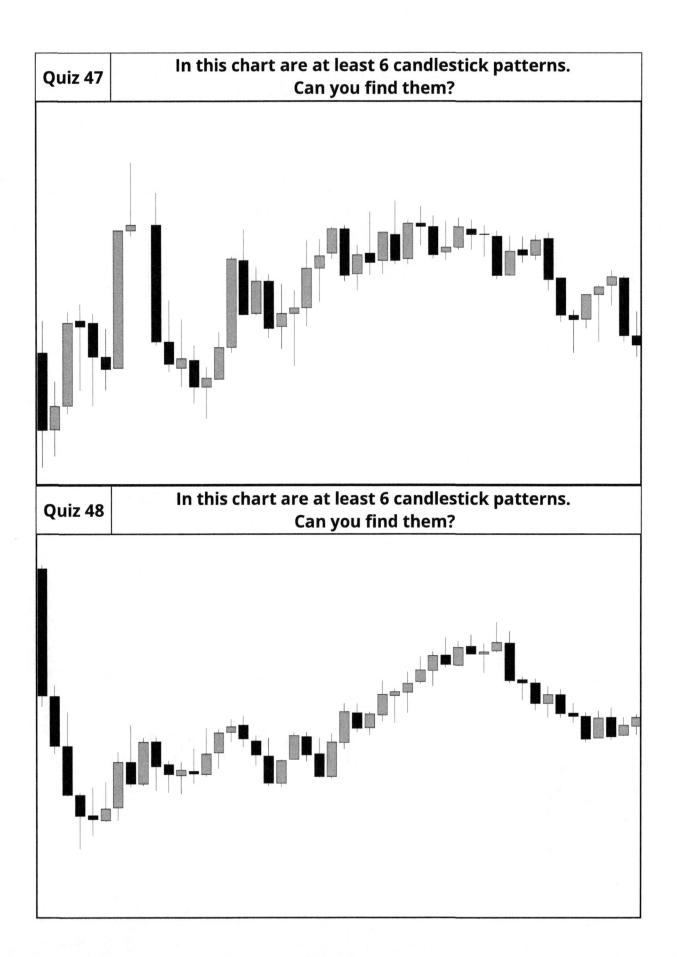

Quiz 48	**In this chart are at least 6 candlestick patterns.** **Can you find them?**

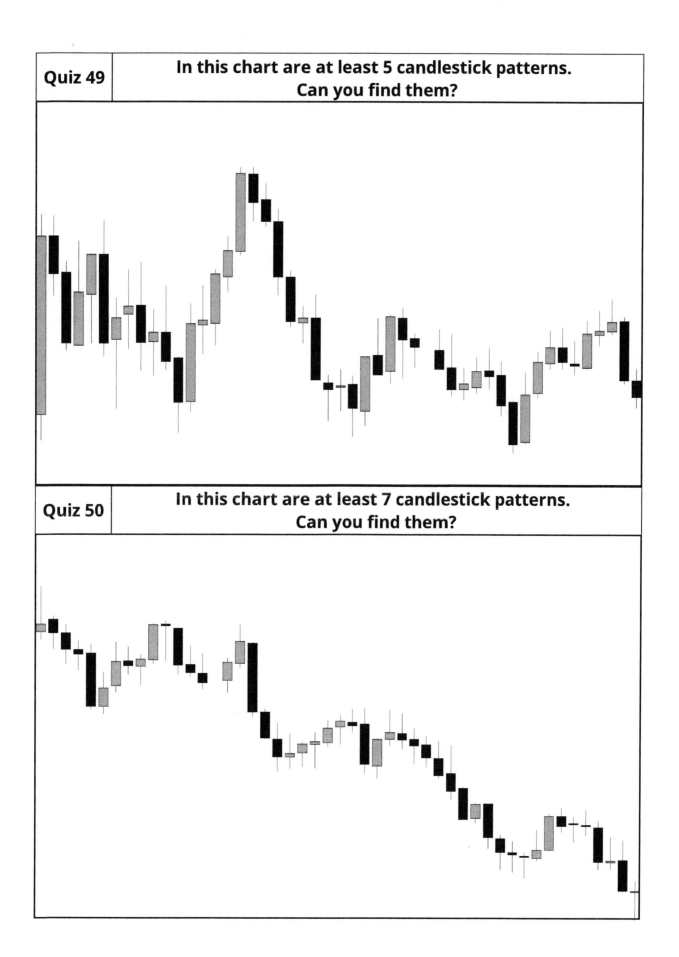

Quiz 49 — In this chart are at least 5 candlestick patterns. Can you find them?

Quiz 50 — In this chart are at least 7 candlestick patterns. Can you find them?

Chapter 5

Answers for Advanced Challenge

Answers for Advanced Challenge

Great job on completing this challenge. The following pages will give you the names of the candlestick patterns and where they were found. Did you find them all? If not you can try again until you have a 100% ... or more if you found additional patterns.

Answers to quiz number	# and name of Candlestick Pattern
Quiz # Answers	1 Bull Flag, 2 Shooting Star, 3 Bearish Tweezer, 4 Hammer, 5 Bullish Tweezer, 6 Bull Flag, 7 Bullish Tweezer

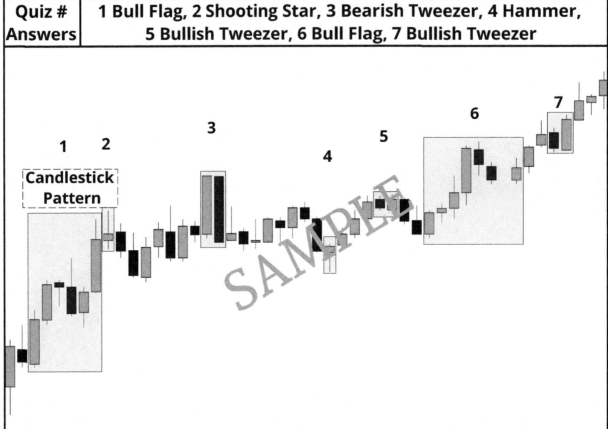

Quiz 1 Answers	1 Bull Flag, 2 Shooting Star, 3 Bearish Tweezer, 4 Hammer, 5 Bullish Tweezer, 6 Bull Flag, 7 Bullish Rickshaw Man

Quiz 2 Answers	1 Three Black Crows, 2 Hammer, 3 Bearish Marubozu, 4 Flat Top Breakout, 5 Shooting Star, 6 Bullish Engulfing Candle

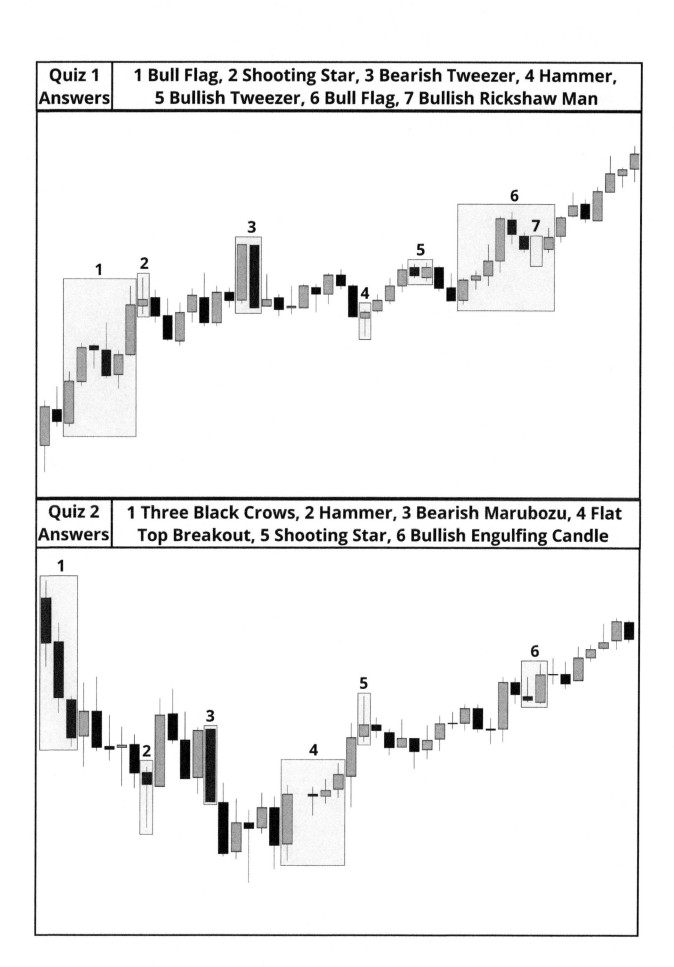

Quiz 3 Answers	1 Shooting Star, 2 Bearish Doji Star, 3 Hanging Man, 4 Hammer, 5 Bullish Rickshaw Man, 6 Three White Soldiers

Quiz 4 Answers	1 Flat Top Breakout, 2 Hammer, 3 Bearish Rickshaw Man, 4 Bearish Tweezer, 5 Inverted Hammer, 6 Hammer

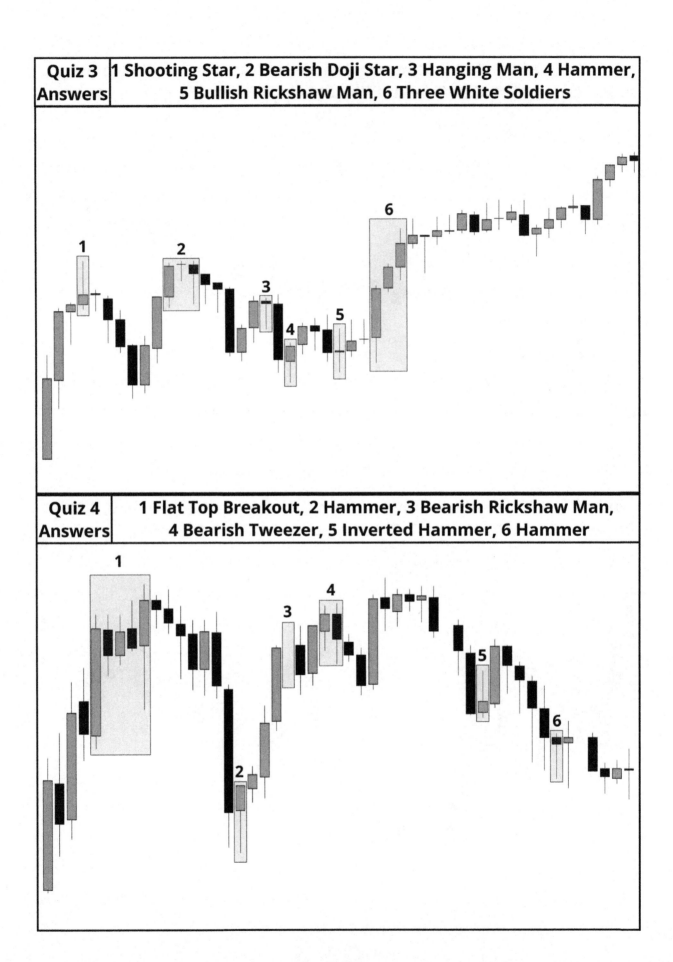

Quiz 5 Answers	1 Bearish Spinning Top, 2 Bearish Tweezer, 3 Hammer, 4 Bearish Doji, 5 Takuri, 6 Bearish Tweezer, 7 Bullish Tweezer

Quiz 6 Answers	1 Bullish Doji, 2 Shooting Star, 3 Bullish Marubosu, 4 Dark Cloud Cover, 5 Hammer, 6 Bearish Tweezer, 7 Hammer

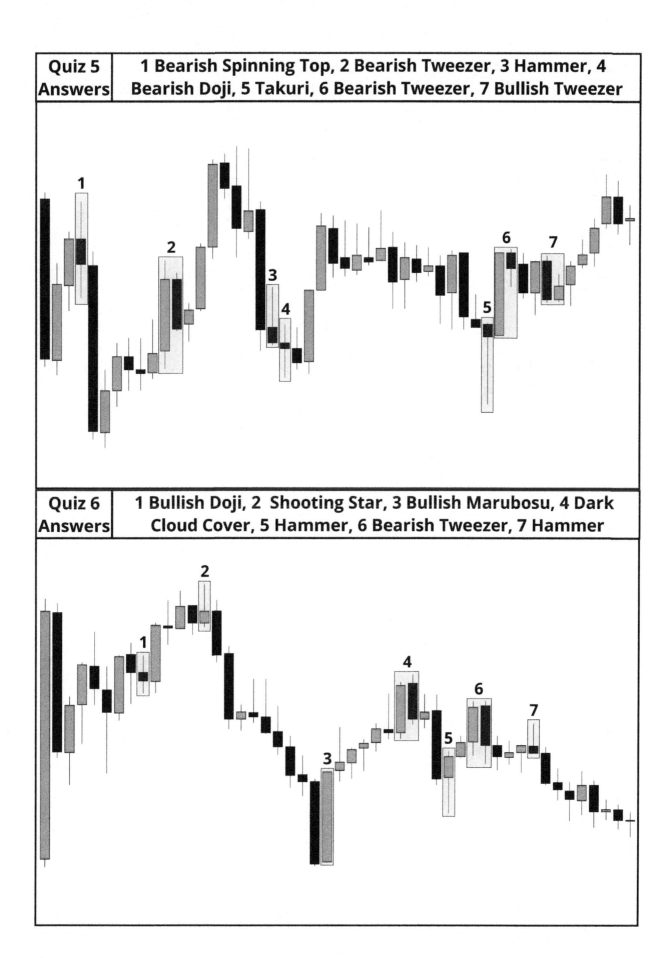

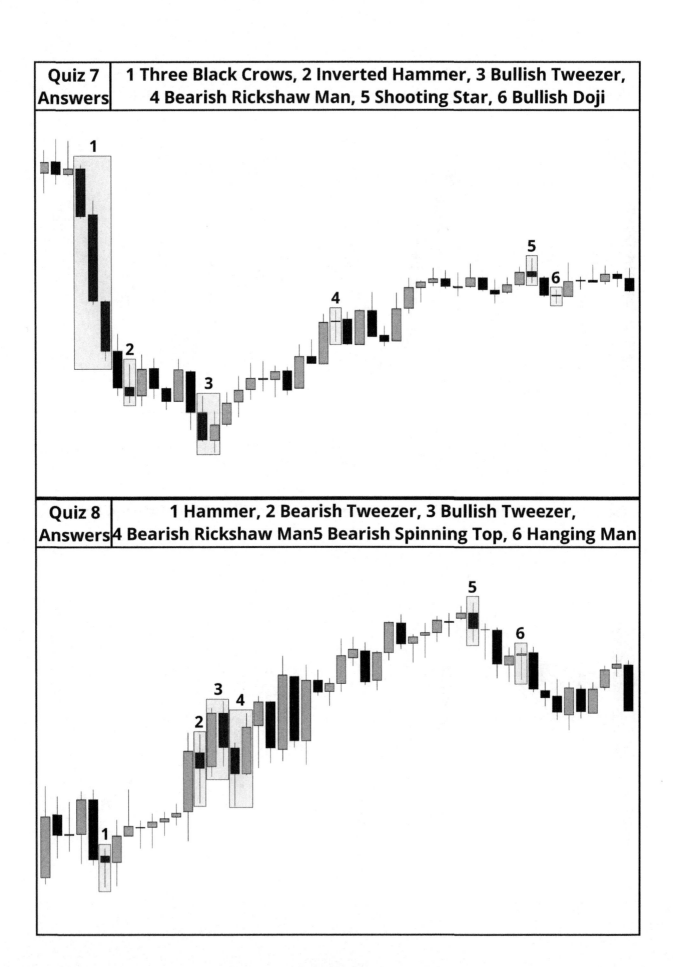

Quiz 7 Answers	1 Three Black Crows, 2 Inverted Hammer, 3 Bullish Tweezer, 4 Bearish Rickshaw Man, 5 Shooting Star, 6 Bullish Doji

Quiz 8 Answers	1 Hammer, 2 Bearish Tweezer, 3 Bullish Tweezer, 4 Bearish Rickshaw Man 5 Bearish Spinning Top, 6 Hanging Man

Quiz 9 Answers	1 Bearish Rickshaw Man, 2 Bearish Spinning Top, 3 Bear Flag, 4 Bullish Tweezer, 5 Bullis Tweezer, 6 Shooting Star

Quiz 10 Answers	1 Three Black Crows, 2 Inverted Hammer 3, Grave Stone, 4 Bearish Marubozu, 5 Dragonfly

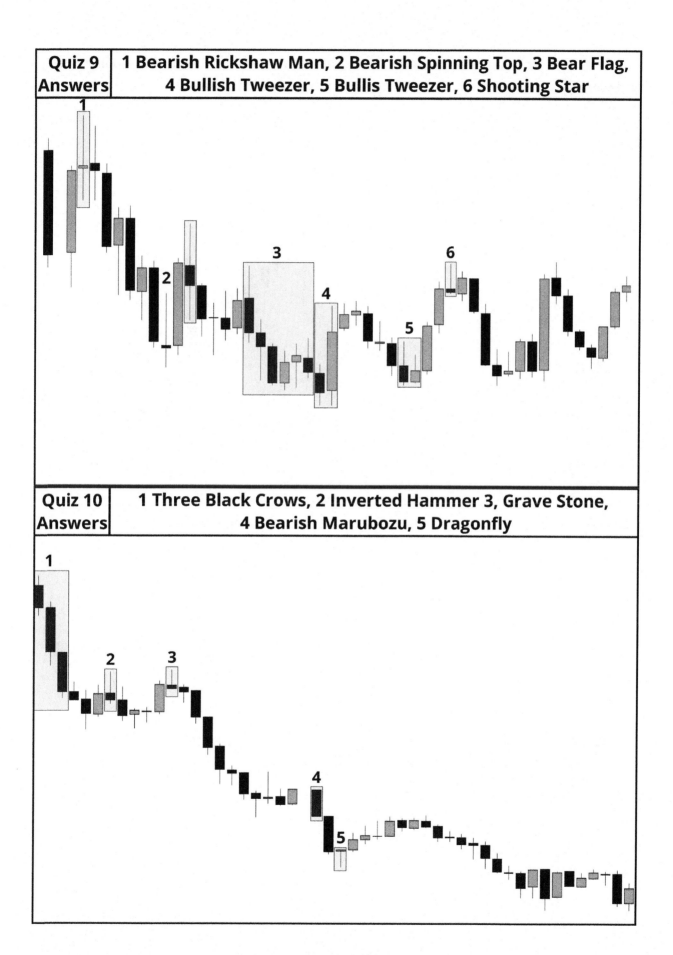

Quiz 11 Answers	1 Bearish Rickshaw Man, 2 Inverted Hammer, 3 Shooting Star, 4 Dragonfly, 5 Bullish Tweezer

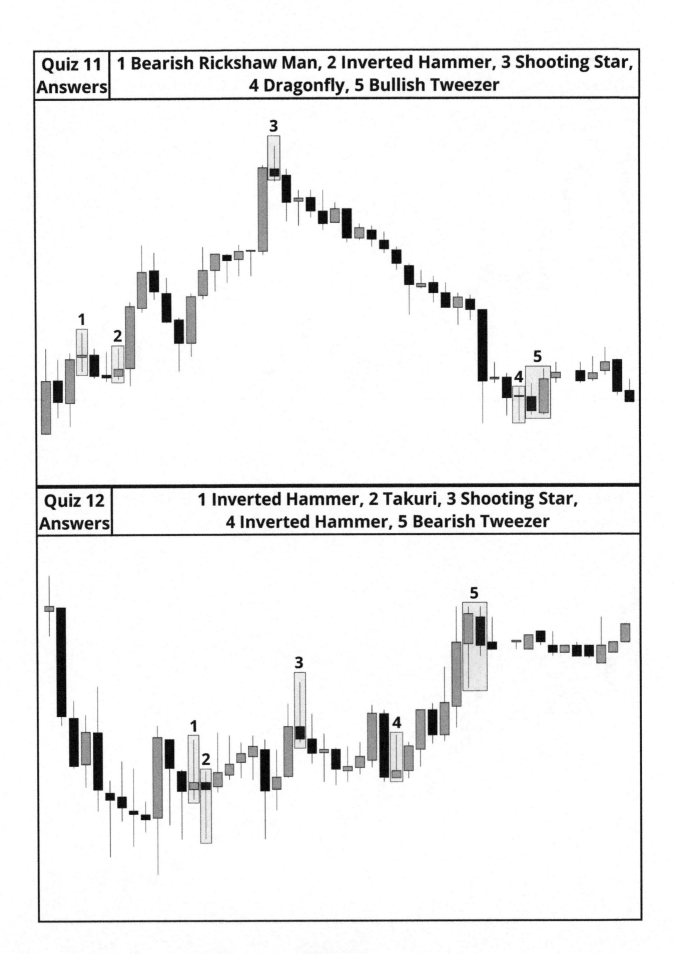

Quiz 12 Answers	1 Inverted Hammer, 2 Takuri, 3 Shooting Star, 4 Inverted Hammer, 5 Bearish Tweezer

Quiz 13 Answers	1 Bear Flag, 2 Morning Star, 3 Shooting Star, 4 Dragonfly, 5 Hanging Man, 6 Dragonfly

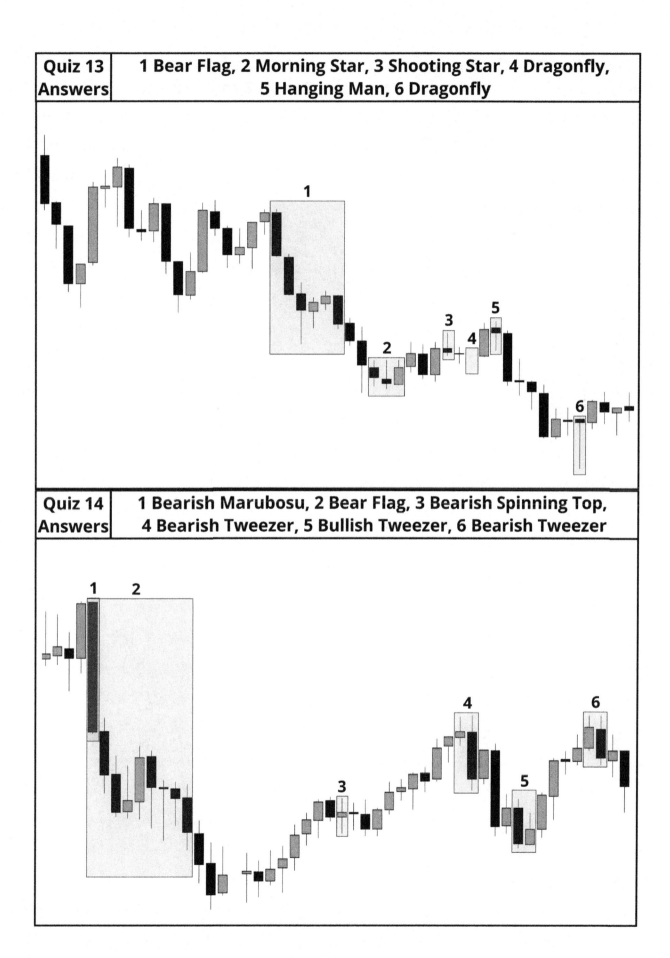

Quiz 14 Answers	1 Bearish Marubosu, 2 Bear Flag, 3 Bearish Spinning Top, 4 Bearish Tweezer, 5 Bullish Tweezer, 6 Bearish Tweezer

Quiz 15 Answers	1 Bullish Spinning Top, 2 Bearish Engulfing Candle, 3 Bullish Tweezer, 4 Shooting Star, 5 Bearish Tweezer

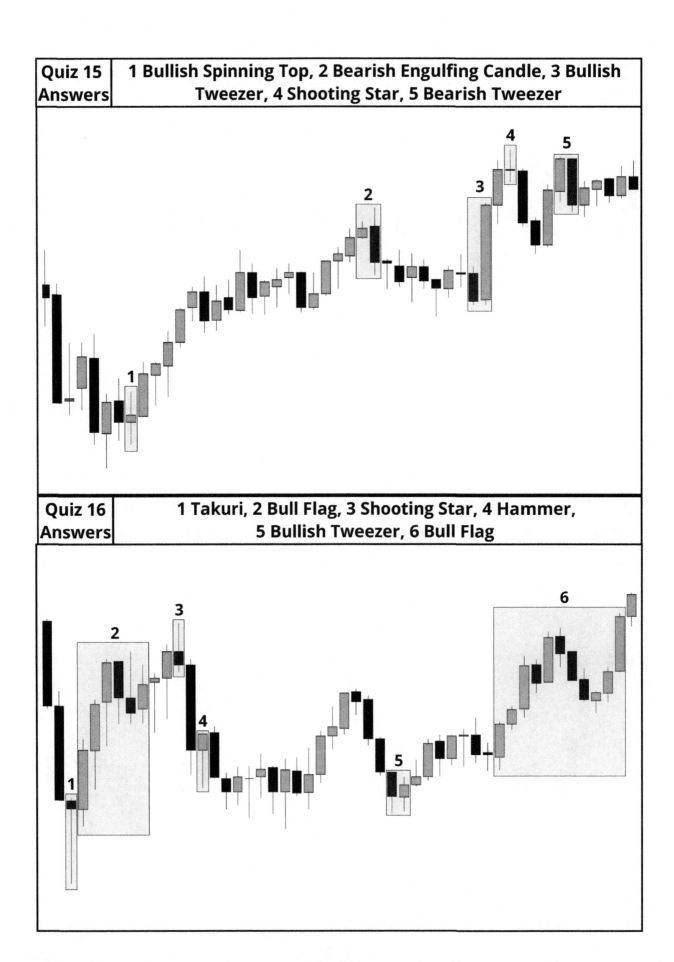

Quiz 16 Answers	1 Takuri, 2 Bull Flag, 3 Shooting Star, 4 Hammer, 5 Bullish Tweezer, 6 Bull Flag

Quiz 17 Answers	1 Bearish Doji, 2 Dragonfly, 3 Bullish Tweezer, 4 Hammer, 5 Bearish Rickshaw Man

Quiz 18 Answers	1 Three White Soldiers, 2 Hanging Man, 3 Hammer, 4 Bearish Doji, 5 Dragonfly, 6 Bull Flag

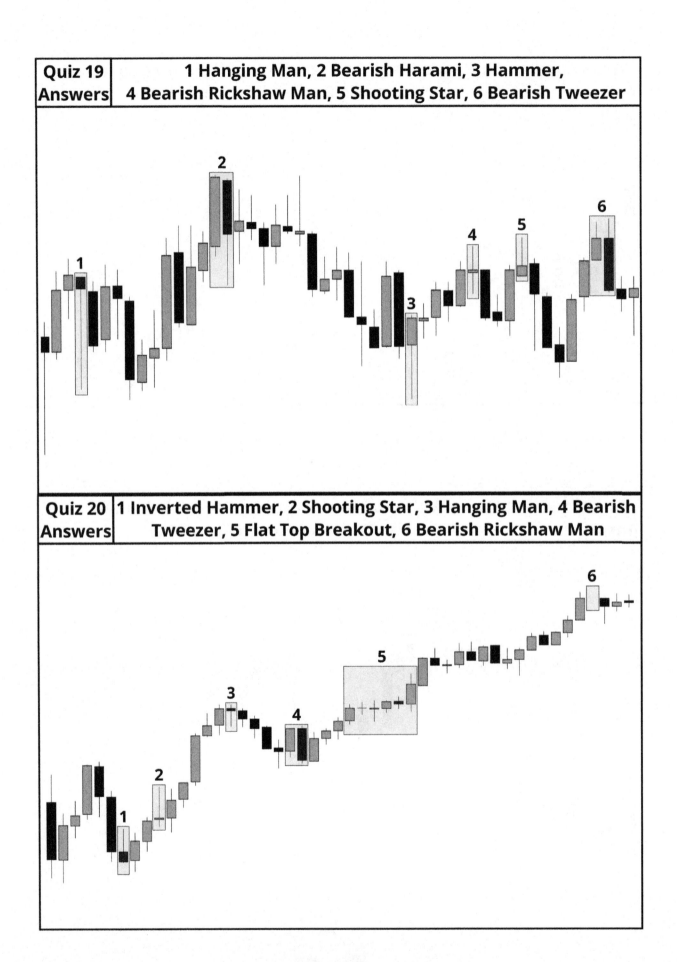

Quiz 19 Answers	1 Hanging Man, 2 Bearish Harami, 3 Hammer, 4 Bearish Rickshaw Man, 5 Shooting Star, 6 Bearish Tweezer

Quiz 20 Answers	1 Inverted Hammer, 2 Shooting Star, 3 Hanging Man, 4 Bearish Tweezer, 5 Flat Top Breakout, 6 Bearish Rickshaw Man

Quiz 21 Answers	1 Shooting Star, 2 Bullish Tweezer, 3 Hanging Man, 4 Hammer, 5 Bearish Spinning Top

Quiz 22 Answers	1 Shooting Star, 2 Hanging Man, 3 Inverted Hammer, 4 Bullish Tweezer, 5 Hanging Man

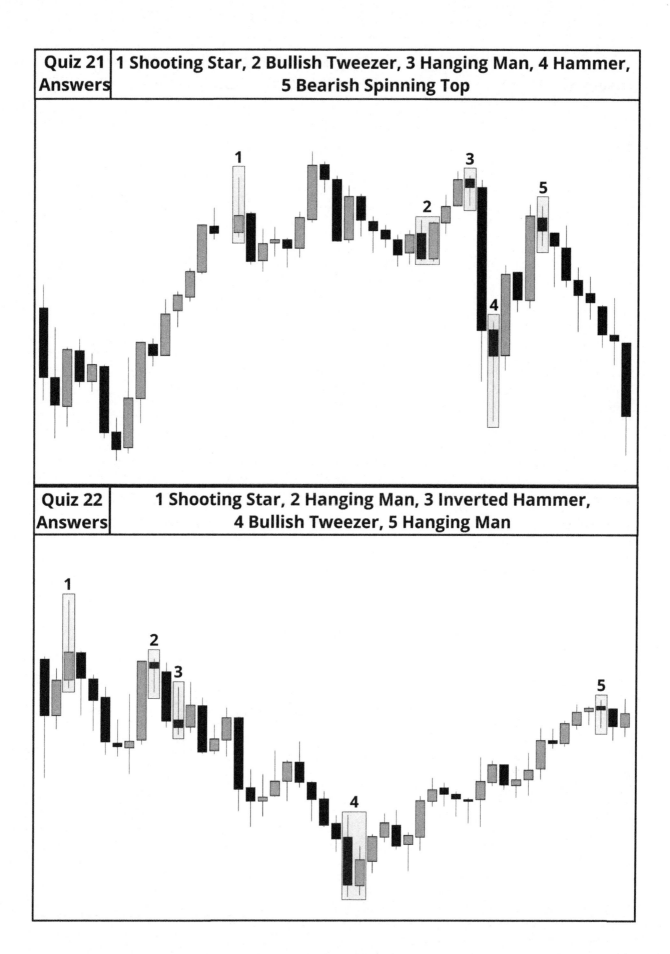

Quiz 23 Answers	1 Bull Flag, 2 Hanging Man, 3 Three White Soldiers, 4 Flat Top Breakout

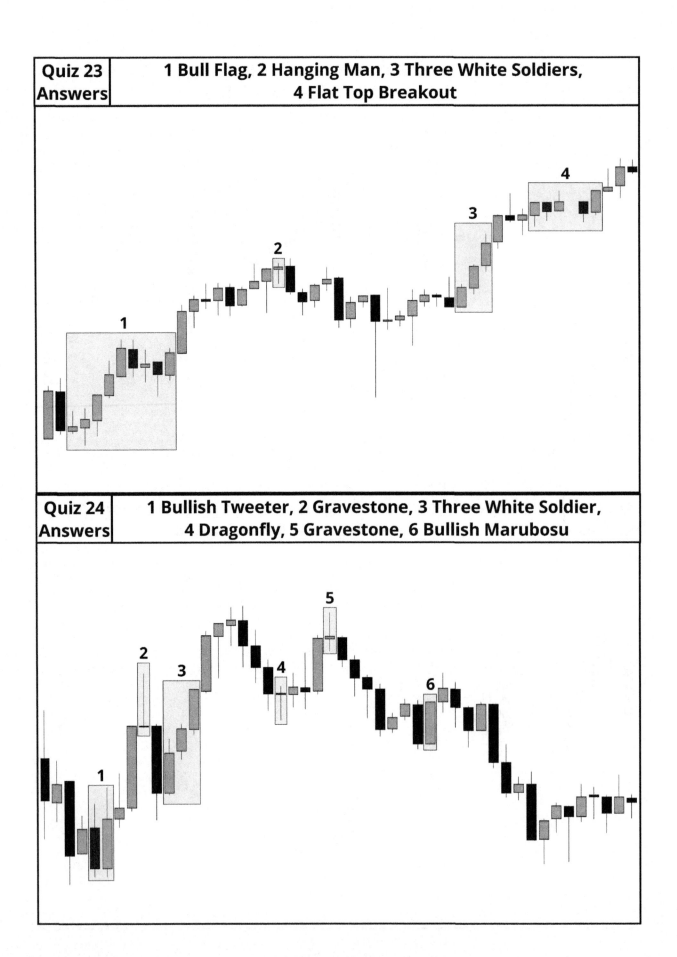

Quiz 24 Answers	1 Bullish Tweeter, 2 Gravestone, 3 Three White Soldier, 4 Dragonfly, 5 Gravestone, 6 Bullish Marubosu

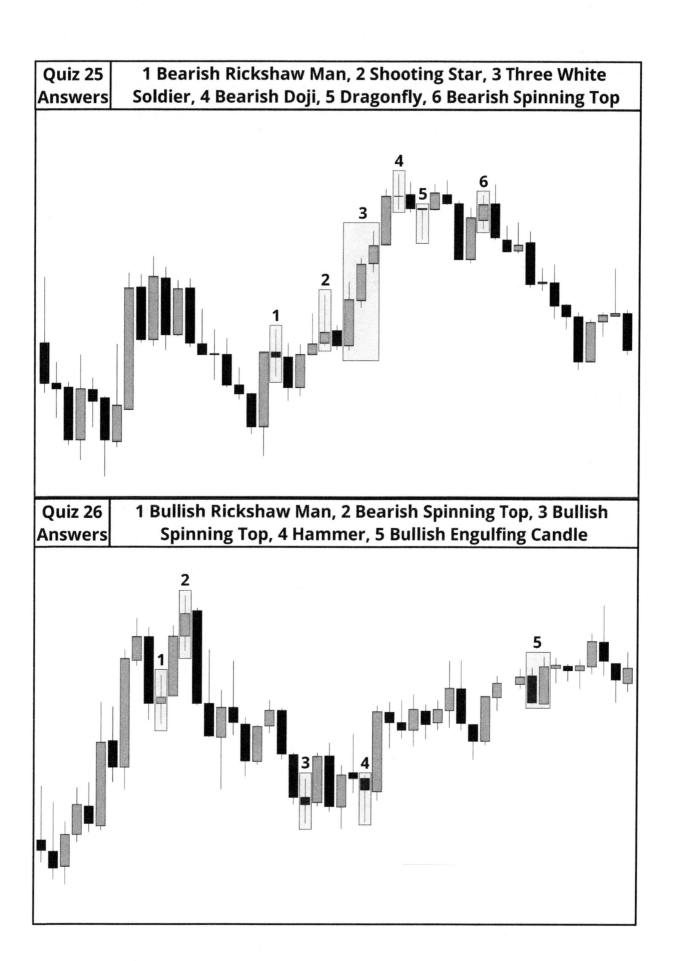

Quiz 25 Answers	1 Bearish Rickshaw Man, 2 Shooting Star, 3 Three White Soldier, 4 Bearish Doji, 5 Dragonfly, 6 Bearish Spinning Top

Quiz 26 Answers	1 Bullish Rickshaw Man, 2 Bearish Spinning Top, 3 Bullish Spinning Top, 4 Hammer, 5 Bullish Engulfing Candle

Quiz 27 Answers	1 Dragonfly, 2 Bullish Tweezer, 3 Hammer, 4 Bearish Doji

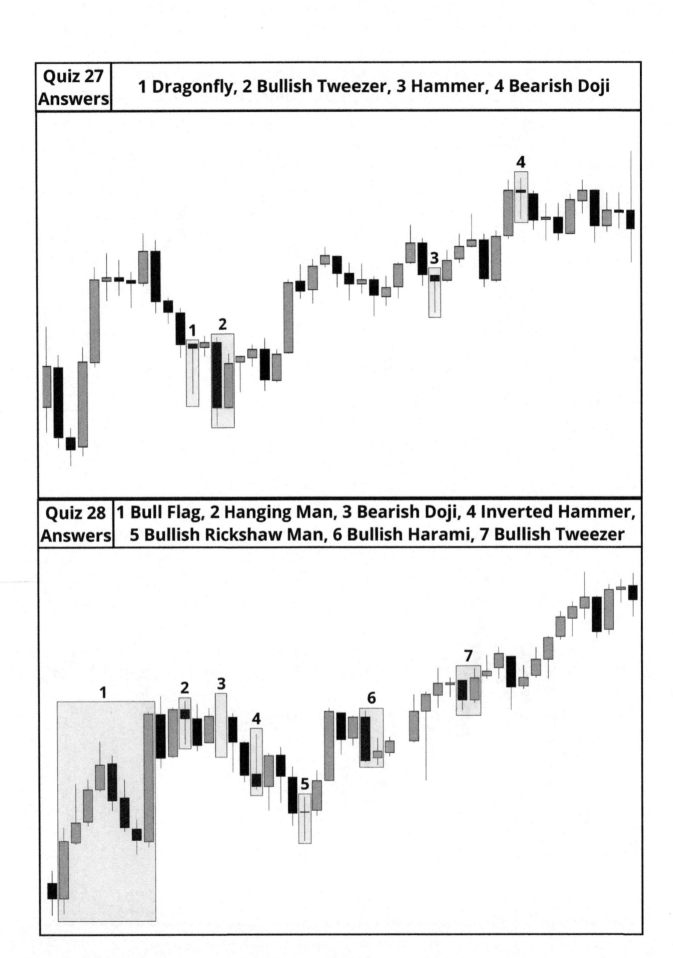

Quiz 28 Answers	1 Bull Flag, 2 Hanging Man, 3 Bearish Doji, 4 Inverted Hammer, 5 Bullish Rickshaw Man, 6 Bullish Harami, 7 Bullish Tweezer

Quiz 29 Answers	1 Three Black Crows, 2 Hammer, 3 Hammer, 4 Hanging Man, 5 Inverted Hammer, 6 Three White Soldiers, 7 Dragonfly

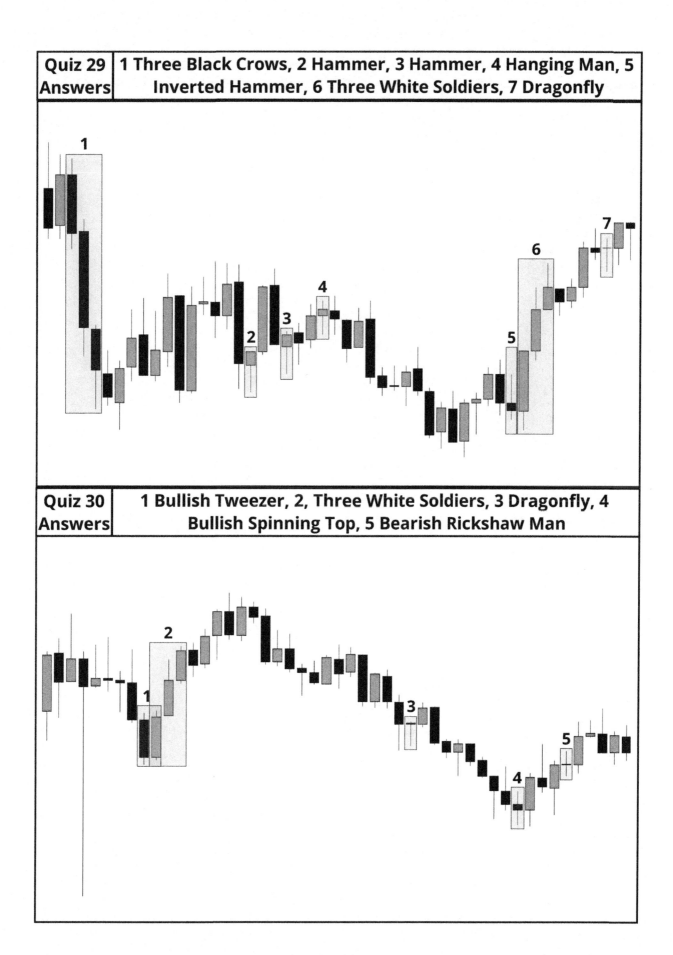

Quiz 30 Answers	1 Bullish Tweezer, 2, Three White Soldiers, 3 Dragonfly, 4 Bullish Spinning Top, 5 Bearish Rickshaw Man

Quiz 31 Answers	1 Bearish Tweezer, 2 Bullish Tweezer, 3 Three Black Crows, 4 Bullish Tweezer, 5 Gravestone, 6 Bearish Marubozu

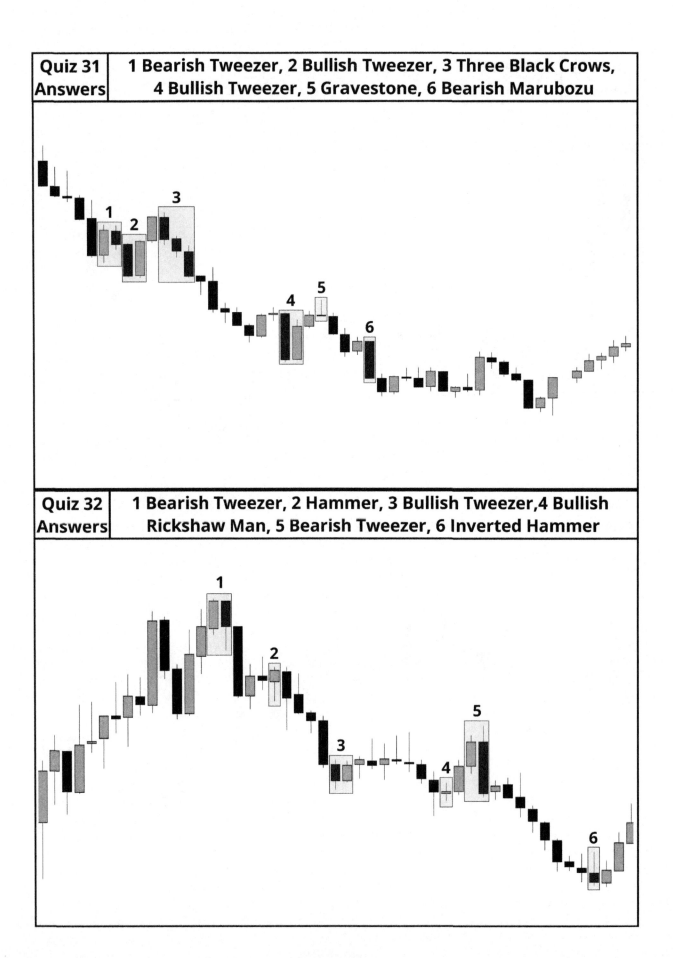

Quiz 32 Answers	1 Bearish Tweezer, 2 Hammer, 3 Bullish Tweezer, 4 Bullish Rickshaw Man, 5 Bearish Tweezer, 6 Inverted Hammer

Quiz 33 Answers	1 Bearish Spinning Top, 2 Bearish Doji, 3 Shooting Star, 4 Bearish Marubozu, 5 Bearish Tweezer, 6 Shooting Star

Quiz 34 Answers	1 Hanging Man, 2 Hanging Man, 3 Bearish Rickshaw man, 4 Flat Top Breakout

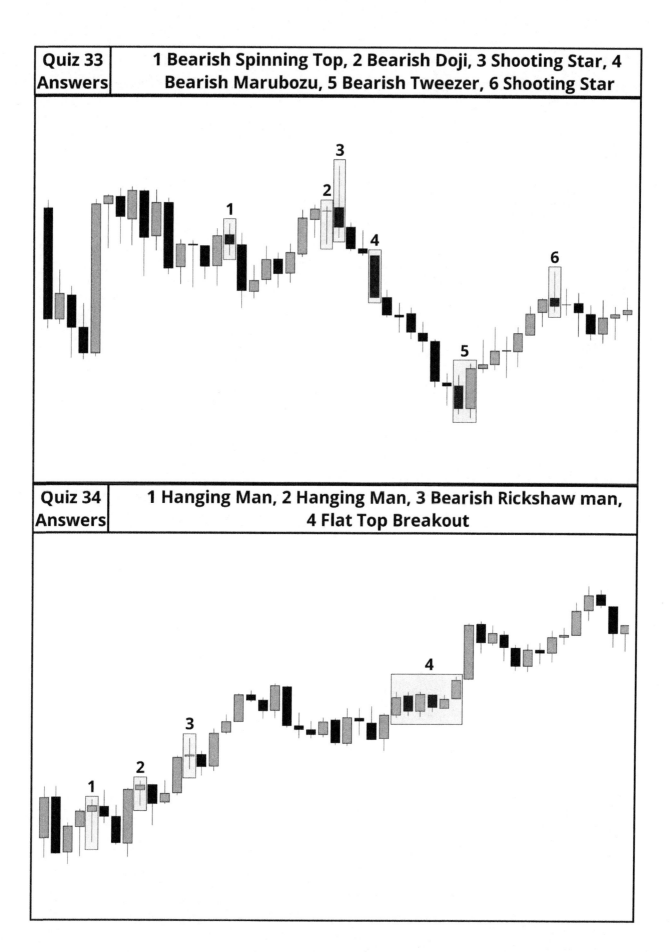

Quiz 35 Answers	1 Bearish Tweezer, 2 Hanging Man, 3 Dragonfly, 4 Bullish Spinning Top, 5 Inverted Hammer, 6 Bullish Rickshaw Man

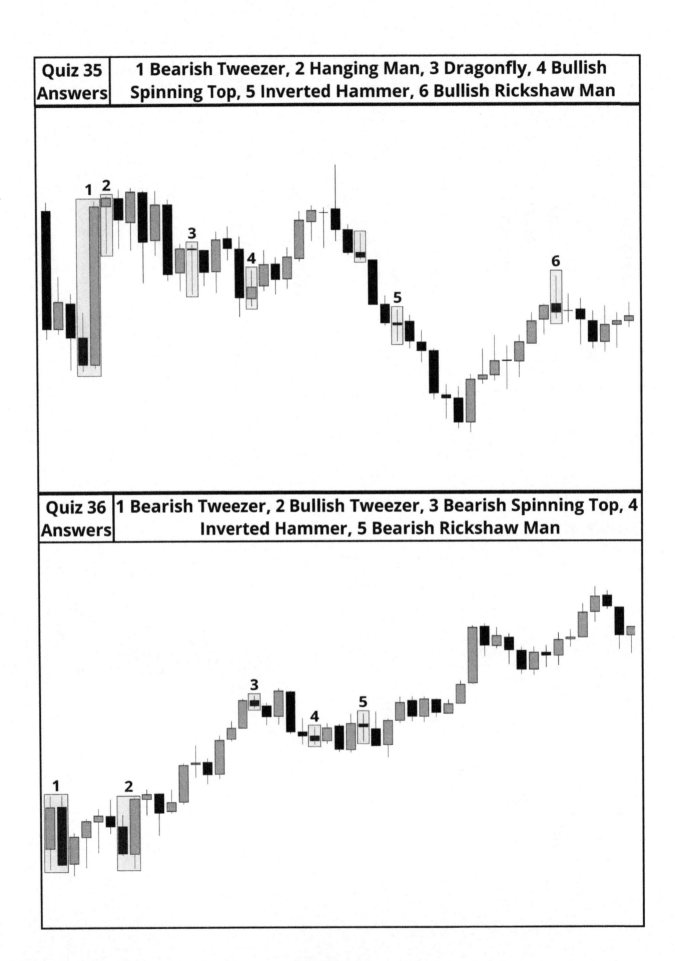

Quiz 36 Answers	1 Bearish Tweezer, 2 Bullish Tweezer, 3 Bearish Spinning Top, 4 Inverted Hammer, 5 Bearish Rickshaw Man

Quiz 37 Answers	1 Shooting Star, 2 Inverted Hammer, 3 Bearish Doji Star, 4 Three Black Crows, 5 Bullish Spinning Top, 6 Hammer

Quiz 38 Answers	1 Inverted Hammer, 2 Hanging Man, 3 Inverted Hammer, 4 Bullish Tweezer, 5 Shooting Star, 6 Bearish Tweezer

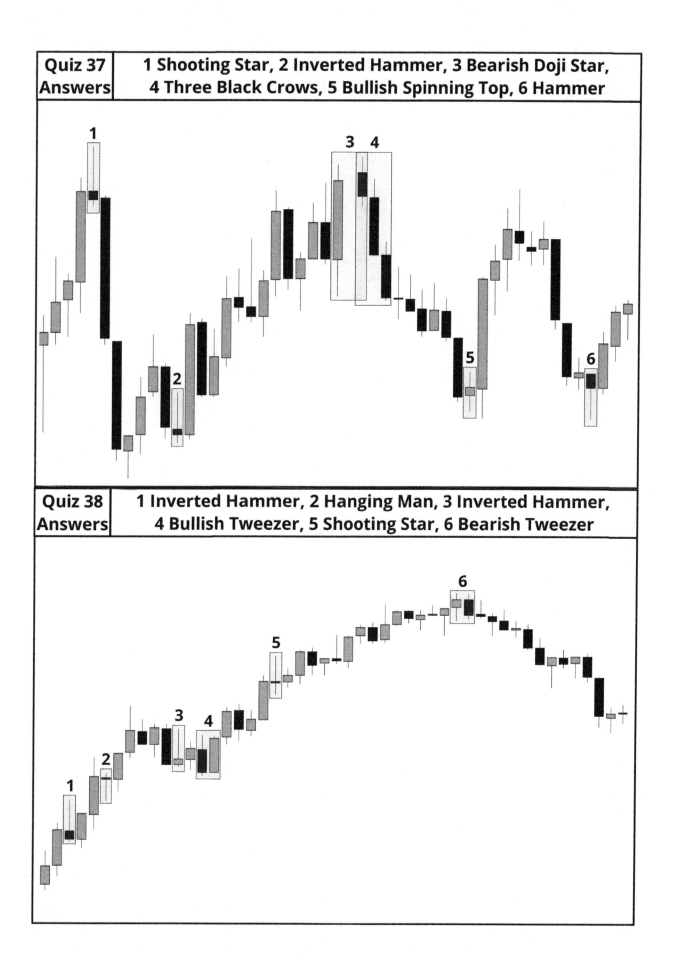

Quiz 39 Answers	1 Shooting Star, 2 Three Black Crows, 3 Morning Star, 4 Bearish Flag, 5 Bullish Harami, 6 Gravestone

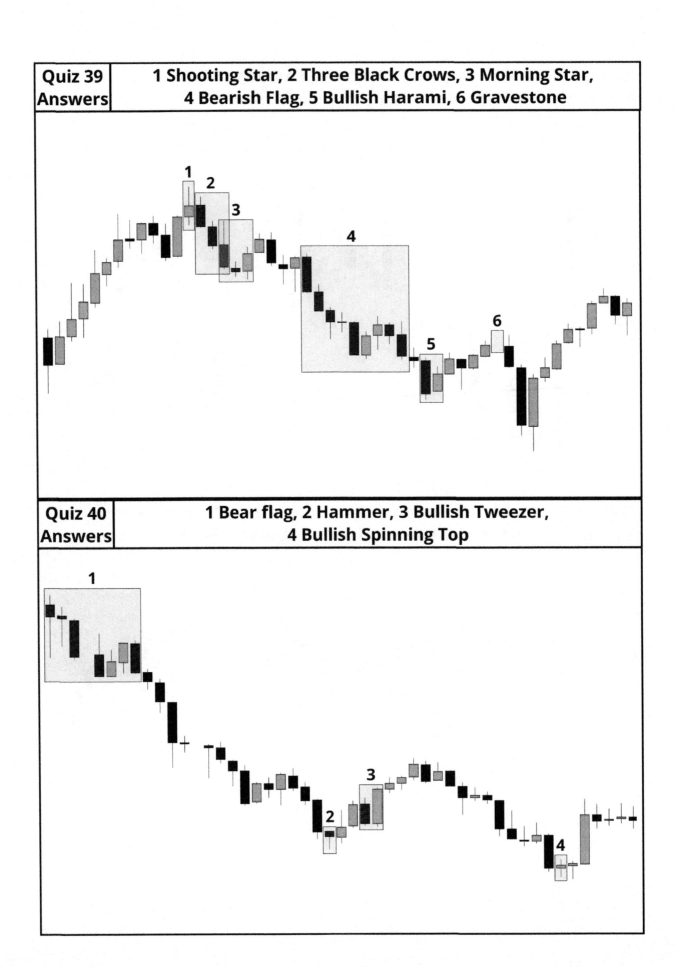

Quiz 40 Answers	1 Bear flag, 2 Hammer, 3 Bullish Tweezer, 4 Bullish Spinning Top

Quiz 41 Answers	1 Bearish Spinning Top, 2 Bullish Rickshaw Man, 3 Bullish Tweezer, 4 Bearish Tweezer, 5 Three Black Crows

Quiz 42 Answers	1 Inverted Hammer, 2 Bullish Flag, 3 Hammer, 4 Gravestone, 5 Shooting Star, 6 Bullish Tweezer

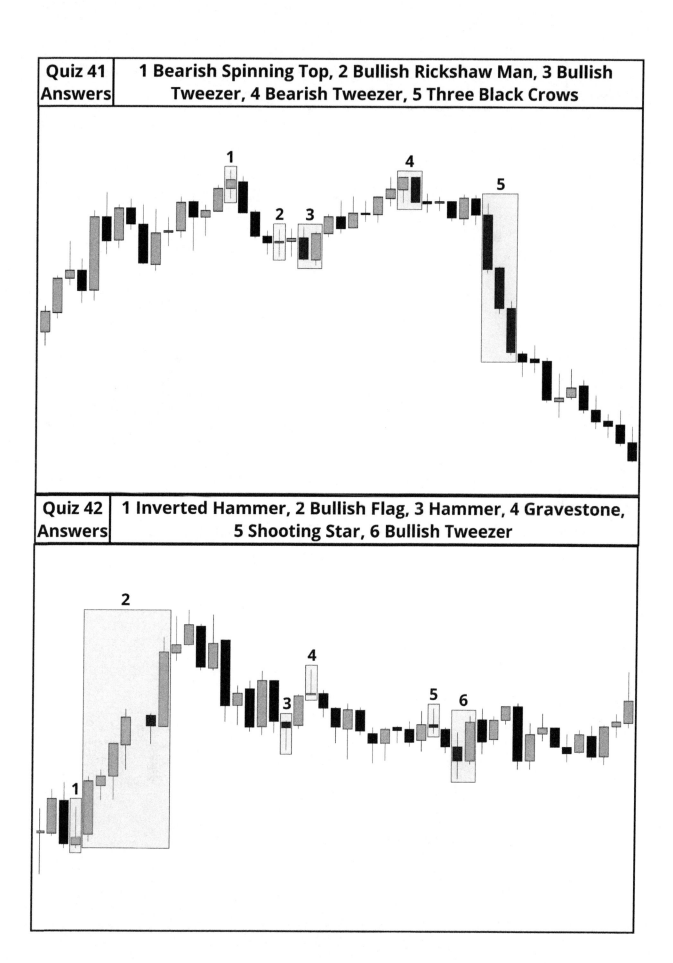

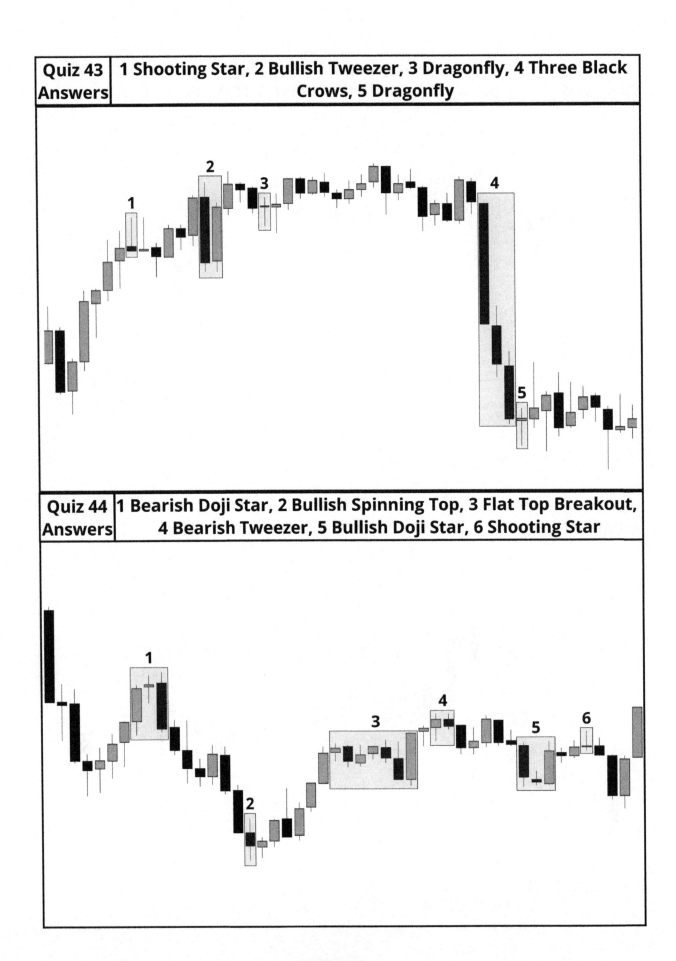

Quiz 43 Answers	1 Shooting Star, 2 Bullish Tweezer, 3 Dragonfly, 4 Three Black Crows, 5 Dragonfly

| Quiz 44 Answers | 1 Bearish Doji Star, 2 Bullish Spinning Top, 3 Flat Top Breakout, 4 Bearish Tweezer, 5 Bullish Doji Star, 6 Shooting Star |

Quiz 45 Answers	1 Dragonfly, 2 Gravestone, 3 Bullish Marubozu, 4 Shooting Star, 5 Bullish Tweezer, 6 Bullish Spinning Top

Quiz 46 Answers	1 Bearish Tweezer, 2 Bullish Tweezer, 3 Bearish Doji, 4 Hanging Man, 5 Bullish Tweezer, 6 Shooting Star

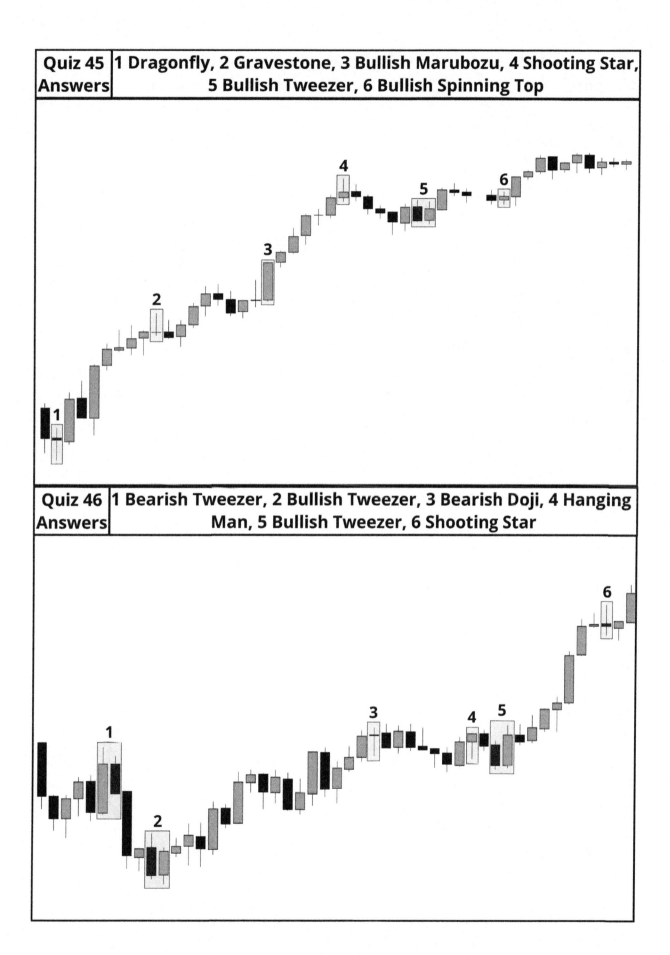

Quiz 47 Answers	1 Bullish Marubozu, 2 Shooting Star, 3 Gravestone, 4 Hammer, 5 Bearish Rickshaw Man, 6 Hammer

Quiz 48 Answers	1 Three Black Crows, 2 Inverted Hammer, 3 Bearish Tweezer, 4 Bullish Tweezer, 5 Bullish Tweezer, 6 Shooting Star

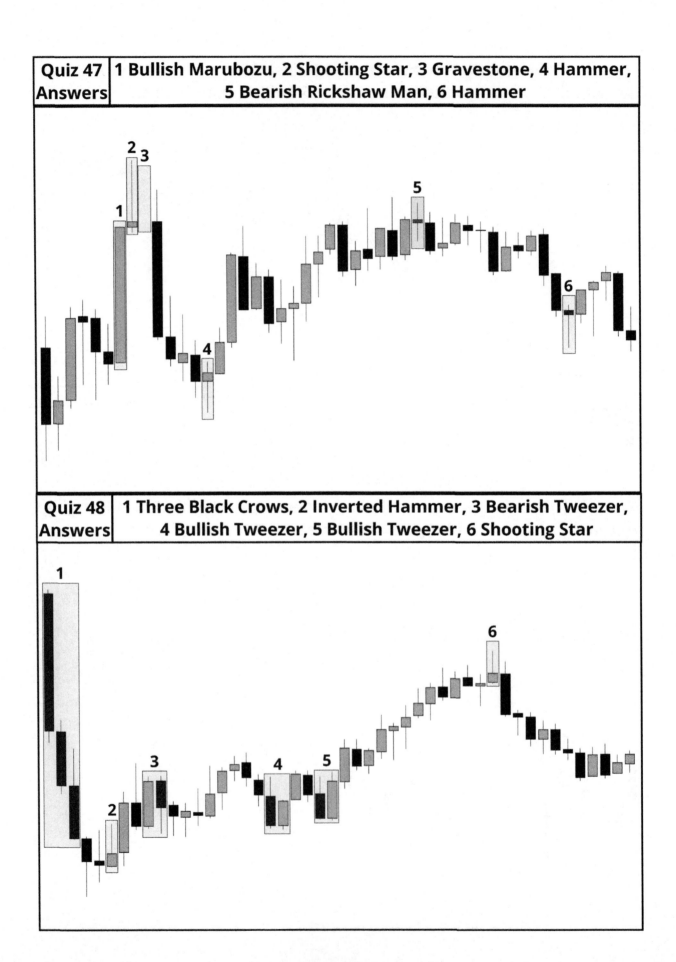

Quiz 49 Answers	1 Bullish Tweezer, 2 Bearish Tweezer, 3 Three Black Crows, 4 Hammer, 5 Bear Flag, 6 Bull Flag, 7 Shooting Star

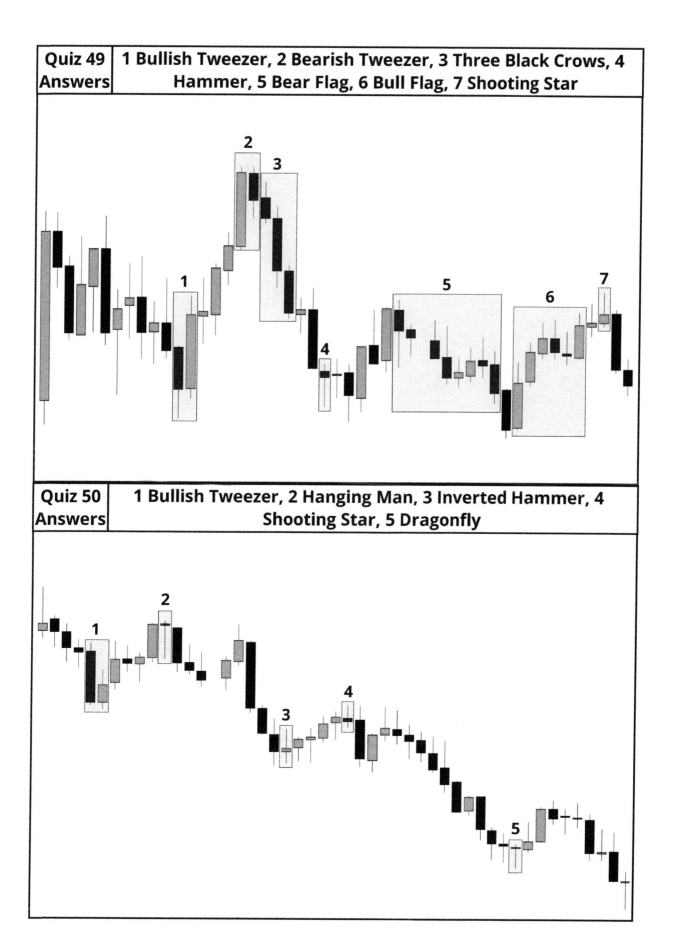

Quiz 50 Answers	1 Bullish Tweezer, 2 Hanging Man, 3 Inverted Hammer, 4 Shooting Star, 5 Dragonfly

Chapter 6

Expert: Two Challenges in One Name and Predict the Direction of the Candlestick Pattern

Name and Predict the Direction
of the Candlestick Pattern

This challenge adds a new twist to candlestick pattern identification. You will see 6 candlestick patterns on each page. At the end of the 12 candles on each chart is a recognizable candlestick pattern that can include 1 or more candlesticks. You must identify the name of the candlestick pattern on the chart section. If you are sure of your choice, can you predict whether the continuation of the candlestick pattern is up or down.

For each of the # groups below determine the candle stick pattern and the direction of the next candlestick to complete the predicted move.

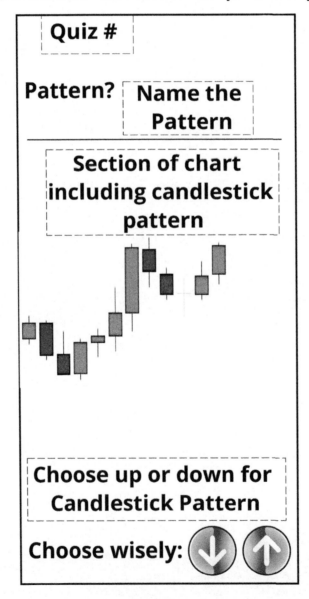

Can You Choose Wisely?

For each of the 6 groups below determine the candle pattern and the direction the next candle should go to complete a successful move.

1	2	3
Pattern?	Pattern?	Pattern?
_____	_____	_____
Choose wisely: ⬇ ⬆	Choose wisely: ⬇ ⬆	Choose wisely: ⬇ ⬆

4	5	6
Pattern?	Pattern?	Pattern?
_____	_____	_____
Choose wisely: ⬇ ⬆	Choose wisely: ⬇ ⬆	Choose wisely: ⬇ ⬆

For each of the 6 groups below determine the candle pattern and the direction the next candle should go to complete a successful move.

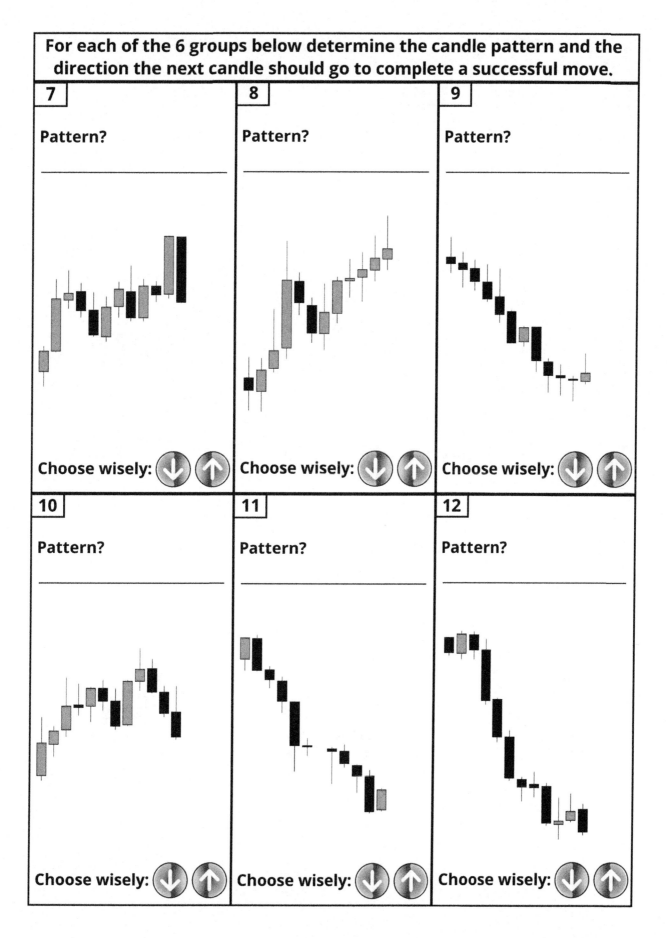

7

Pattern?

_____

Choose wisely: ↓ ↑

8

Pattern?

_____

Choose wisely: ↓ ↑

9

Pattern?

_____

Choose wisely: ↓ ↑

10

Pattern?

_____

Choose wisely: ↓ ↑

11

Pattern?

_____

Choose wisely: ↓ ↑

12

Pattern?

_____

Choose wisely: ↓ ↑

For each of the 6 groups below determine the candle pattern and the direction the next candle should go to complete a successful move.

13

Pattern?

_____

Choose wisely: ⬇ ⬆

14

Pattern?

_____

Choose wisely: ⬇ ⬆

15

Pattern?

_____

Choose wisely: ⬇ ⬆

16

Pattern?

_____

Choose wisely: ⬇ ⬆

17

Pattern?

_____

Choose wisely: ⬇ ⬆

18

Pattern?

_____

Choose wisely: ⬇ ⬆

For each of the 6 groups below determine the candle pattern and the direction the next candle should go to complete a successful move.

19

Pattern?

_____

Choose wisely: ↓ ↑

20

Pattern?

_____

Choose wisely: ↓ ↑

21

Pattern?

_____

Choose wisely: ↓ ↑

22

Pattern?

_____

Choose wisely: ↓ ↑

23

Pattern?

_____

Choose wisely: ↓ ↑

24

Pattern?

_____

Choose wisely: ↓ ↑

For each of the 6 groups below determine the candle pattern and the direction the next candle should go to complete a successful move.

25	26	27
Pattern?	Pattern?	Pattern?
_____	_____	_____
Choose wisely: ⬇ ⬆	Choose wisely: ⬇ ⬆	Choose wisely: ⬇ ⬆

28	29	30
Pattern?	Pattern?	Pattern?
_____	_____	_____
Choose wisely: ⬇ ⬆	Choose wisely: ⬇ ⬆	Choose wisely: ⬇ ⬆

For each of the 6 groups below determine the candle pattern and the direction the next candle should go to complete a successful move.

31

Pattern?

_____

Choose wisely: ↓ ↑

32

Pattern?

_____

Choose wisely: ↓ ↑

33

Pattern?

_____

Choose wisely: ↓ ↑

34

Pattern?

_____

Choose wisely: ↓ ↑

35

Pattern?

_____

Choose wisely: ↓ ↑

36

Pattern?

_____

Choose wisely: ↓ ↑

For each of the 6 groups below determine the candle pattern and the direction the next candle should go to complete a successful move.

37

Pattern?

_____

Choose wisely: ↓ ↑

38

Pattern?

_____

Choose wisely: ↓ ↑

39

Pattern?

_____

Choose wisely: ↓ ↑

40

Pattern?

_____

Choose wisely: ↓ ↑

41

Pattern?

_____

Choose wisely: ↓ ↑

42

Pattern?

_____

Choose wisely: ↓ ↑

For each of the 6 groups below determine the candle pattern and the direction the next candle should go to complete a successful move.

43

Pattern?

_____

Choose wisely: ⬇ ⬆

44

Pattern?

_____

Choose wisely: ⬇ ⬆

45

Pattern?

_____

Choose wisely: ⬇ ⬆

46

Pattern?

_____

Choose wisely: ⬇ ⬆

47

Pattern?

_____

Choose wisely: ⬇ ⬆

48

Pattern?

_____

Choose wisely: ⬇ ⬆

Chapter 7

Answers for Expert Challenge

Answers for Expert Challenge

Completing this challenge will have tested your recognition, naming, and signal of candlestick patterns for trading. Repeat as you need to to give yourself a 100% success.

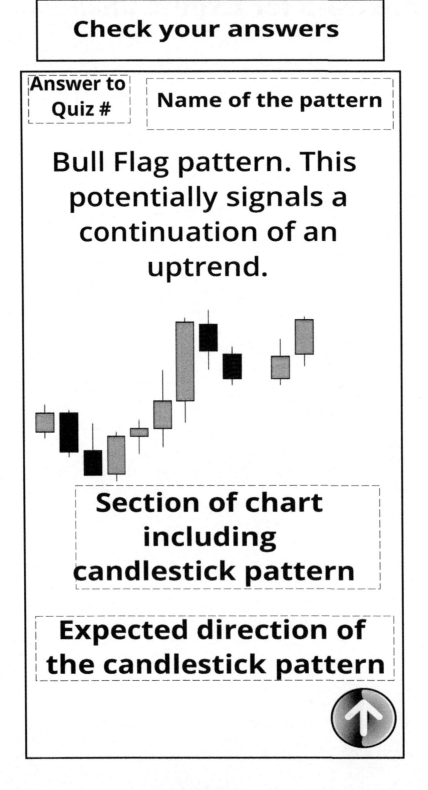

Check your answers

Answer to Quiz #

Name of the pattern

Bull Flag pattern. This potentially signals a continuation of an uptrend.

Section of chart including candlestick pattern

Expected direction of the candlestick pattern

How did you do?

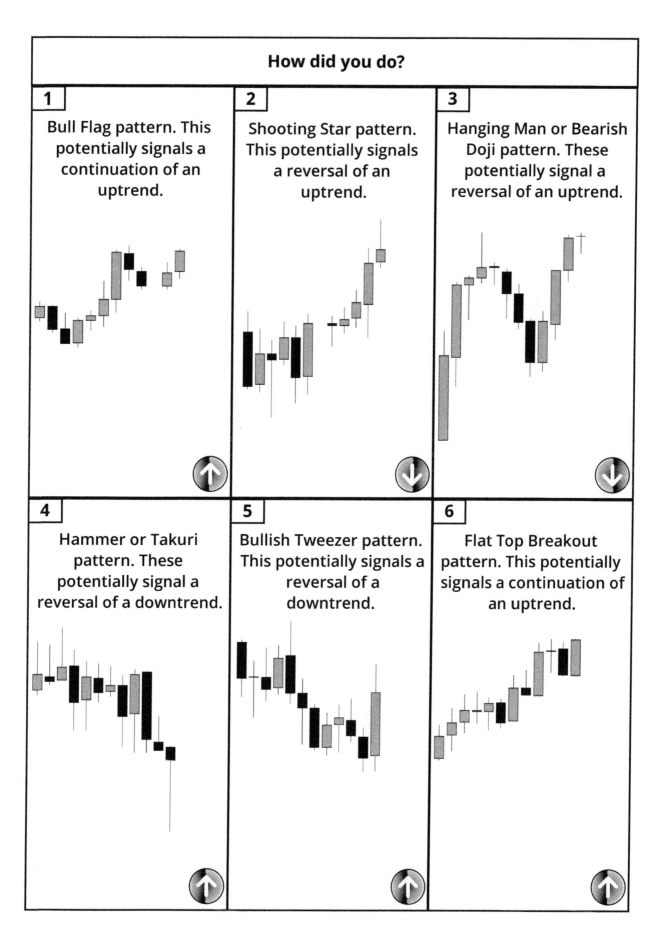

1 Bull Flag pattern. This potentially signals a continuation of an uptrend.

2 Shooting Star pattern. This potentially signals a reversal of an uptrend.

3 Hanging Man or Bearish Doji pattern. These potentially signal a reversal of an uptrend.

4 Hammer or Takuri pattern. These potentially signal a reversal of a downtrend.

5 Bullish Tweezer pattern. This potentially signals a reversal of a downtrend.

6 Flat Top Breakout pattern. This potentially signals a continuation of an uptrend.

How did you do?

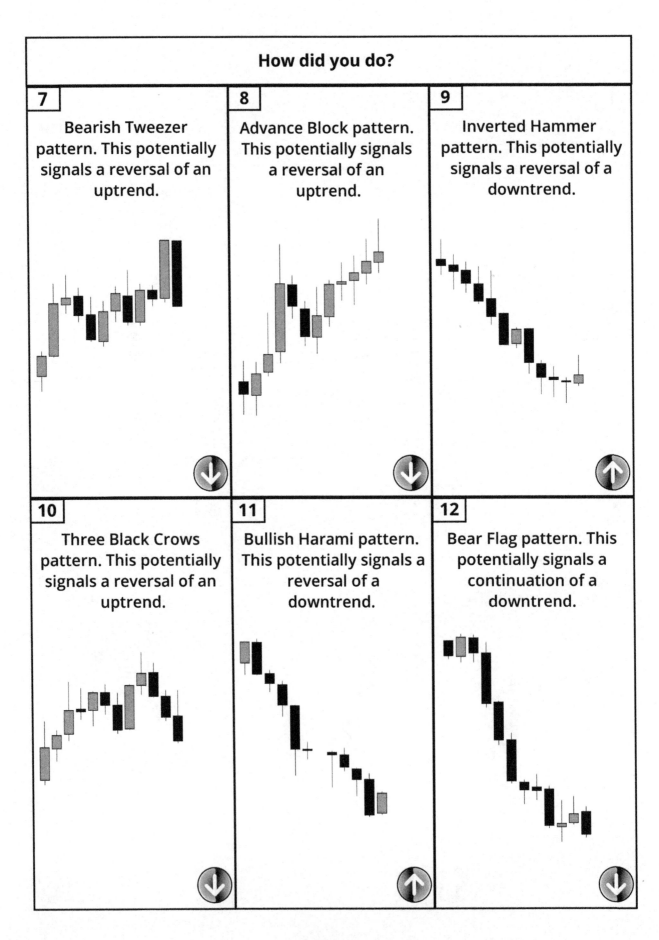

7

Bearish Tweezer pattern. This potentially signals a reversal of an uptrend.

8

Advance Block pattern. This potentially signals a reversal of an uptrend.

9

Inverted Hammer pattern. This potentially signals a reversal of a downtrend.

10

Three Black Crows pattern. This potentially signals a reversal of an uptrend.

11

Bullish Harami pattern. This potentially signals a reversal of a downtrend.

12

Bear Flag pattern. This potentially signals a continuation of a downtrend.

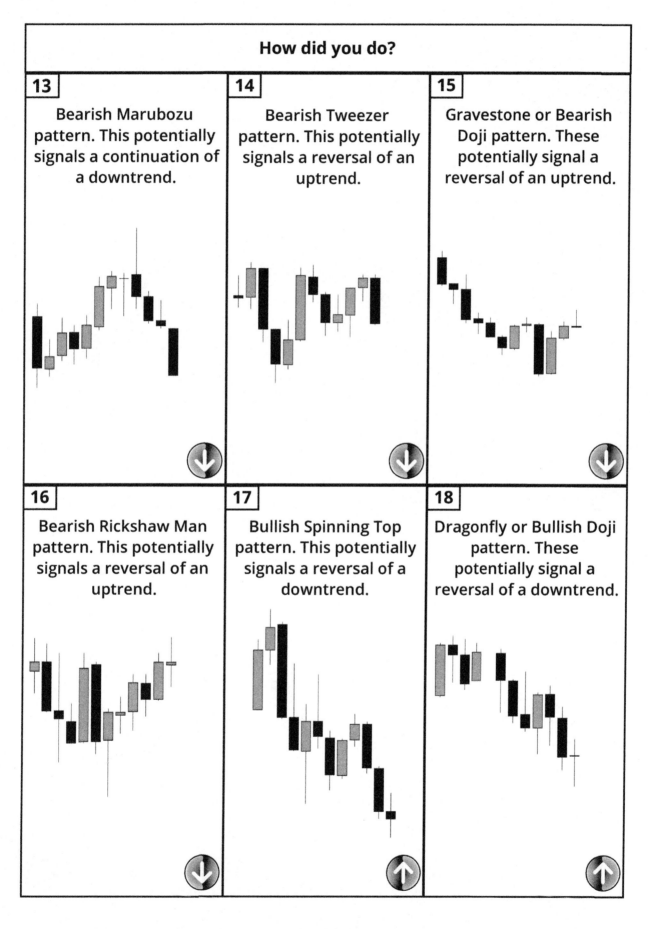

13

Bearish Marubozu pattern. This potentially signals a continuation of a downtrend.

14

Bearish Tweezer pattern. This potentially signals a reversal of an uptrend.

15

Gravestone or Bearish Doji pattern. These potentially signal a reversal of an uptrend.

16

Bearish Rickshaw Man pattern. This potentially signals a reversal of an uptrend.

17

Bullish Spinning Top pattern. This potentially signals a reversal of a downtrend.

18

Dragonfly or Bullish Doji pattern. These potentially signal a reversal of a downtrend.

How did you do?

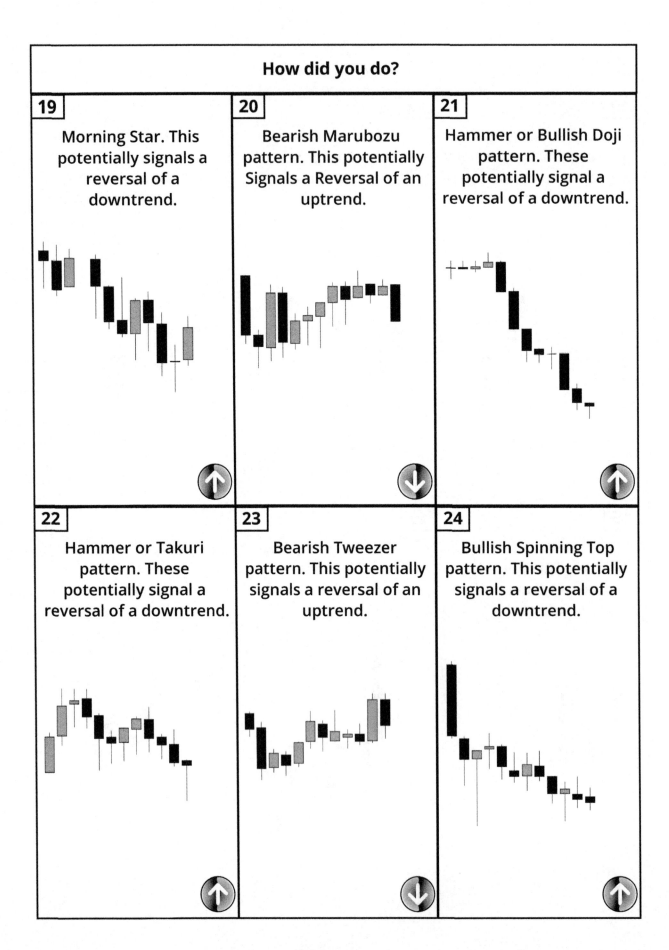

19 Morning Star. This potentially signals a reversal of a downtrend.

20 Bearish Marubozu pattern. This potentially Signals a Reversal of an uptrend.

21 Hammer or Bullish Doji pattern. These potentially signal a reversal of a downtrend.

22 Hammer or Takuri pattern. These potentially signal a reversal of a downtrend.

23 Bearish Tweezer pattern. This potentially signals a reversal of an uptrend.

24 Bullish Spinning Top pattern. This potentially signals a reversal of a downtrend.

How did you do?

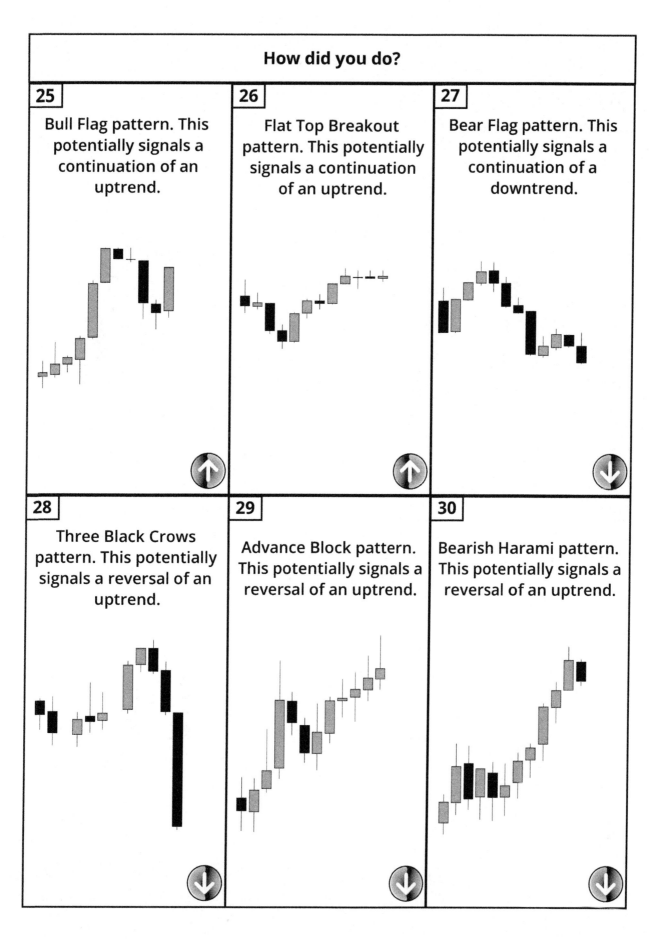

25
Bull Flag pattern. This potentially signals a continuation of an uptrend.

26
Flat Top Breakout pattern. This potentially signals a continuation of an uptrend.

27
Bear Flag pattern. This potentially signals a continuation of a downtrend.

28
Three Black Crows pattern. This potentially signals a reversal of an uptrend.

29
Advance Block pattern. This potentially signals a reversal of an uptrend.

30
Bearish Harami pattern. This potentially signals a reversal of an uptrend.

How did you do?

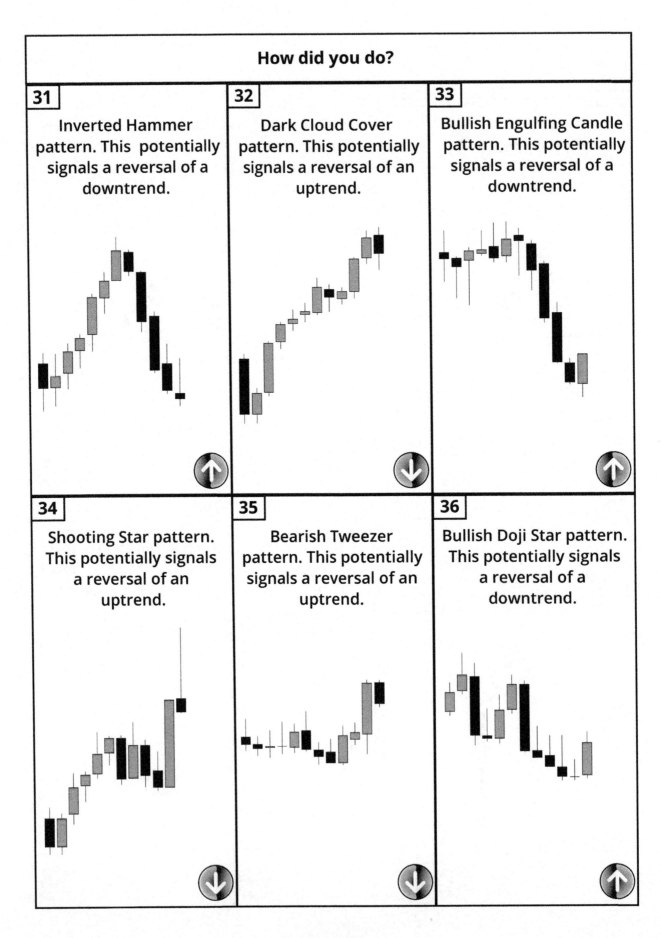

31

Inverted Hammer pattern. This potentially signals a reversal of a downtrend.

32

Dark Cloud Cover pattern. This potentially signals a reversal of an uptrend.

33

Bullish Engulfing Candle pattern. This potentially signals a reversal of a downtrend.

34

Shooting Star pattern. This potentially signals a reversal of an uptrend.

35

Bearish Tweezer pattern. This potentially signals a reversal of an uptrend.

36

Bullish Doji Star pattern. This potentially signals a reversal of a downtrend.

How did you do?

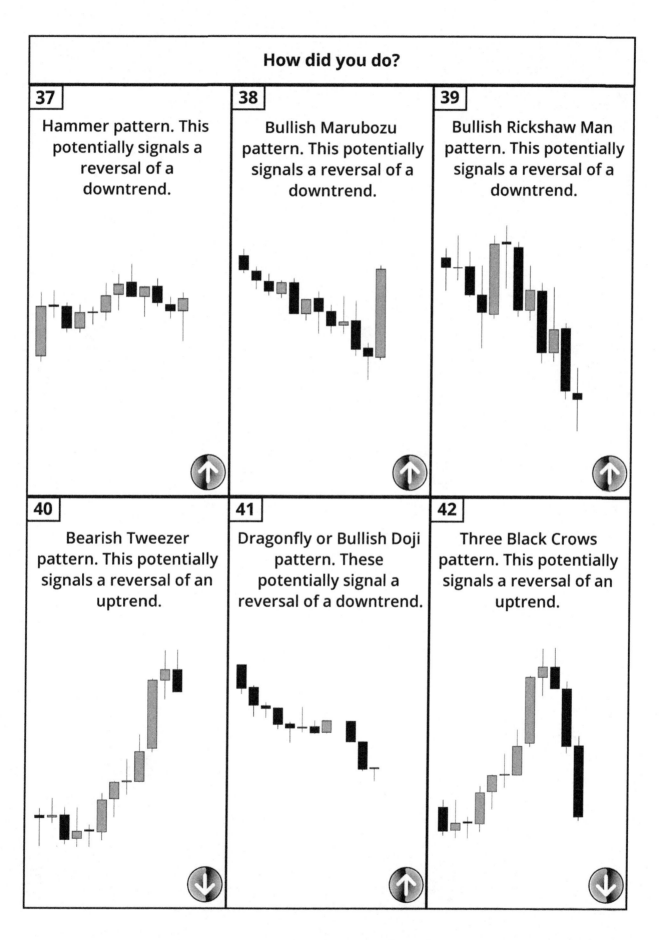

37 Hammer pattern. This potentially signals a reversal of a downtrend.

38 Bullish Marubozu pattern. This potentially signals a reversal of a downtrend.

39 Bullish Rickshaw Man pattern. This potentially signals a reversal of a downtrend.

40 Bearish Tweezer pattern. This potentially signals a reversal of an uptrend.

41 Dragonfly or Bullish Doji pattern. These potentially signal a reversal of a downtrend.

42 Three Black Crows pattern. This potentially signals a reversal of an uptrend.

How did you do?

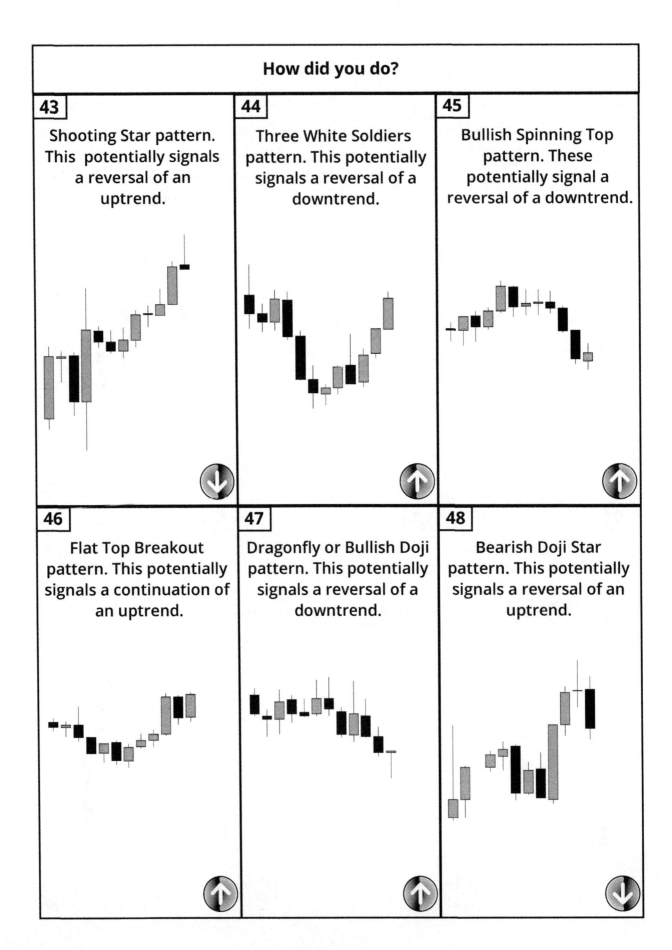

43

Shooting Star pattern. This potentially signals a reversal of an uptrend.

44

Three White Soldiers pattern. This potentially signals a reversal of a downtrend.

45

Bullish Spinning Top pattern. These potentially signal a reversal of a downtrend.

46

Flat Top Breakout pattern. This potentially signals a continuation of an uptrend.

47

Dragonfly or Bullish Doji pattern. This potentially signals a reversal of a downtrend.

48

Bearish Doji Star pattern. This potentially signals a reversal of an uptrend.

Did You Choose Wisely?

Chapter 8

Professional Challenge

Name all the Candlestick Patterns

Name All the Candlestick Patterns

The professional Challenge is a test of memory. 64 candlestick patterns from the first chapter of this book have been shuffled and put into groups of 8. Can you correctly identify all of the candlestick patterns without looking back?

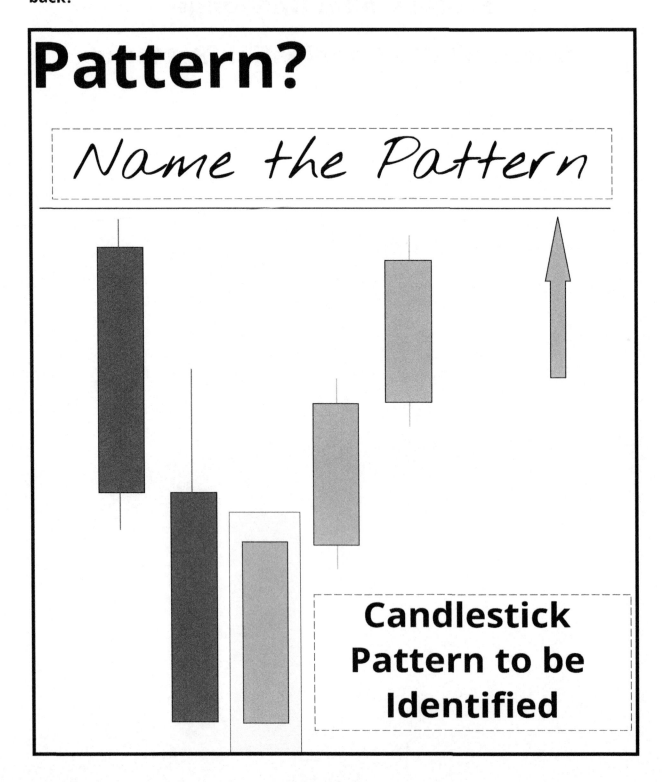

Pattern?

Name the Pattern

Candlestick Pattern to be Identified

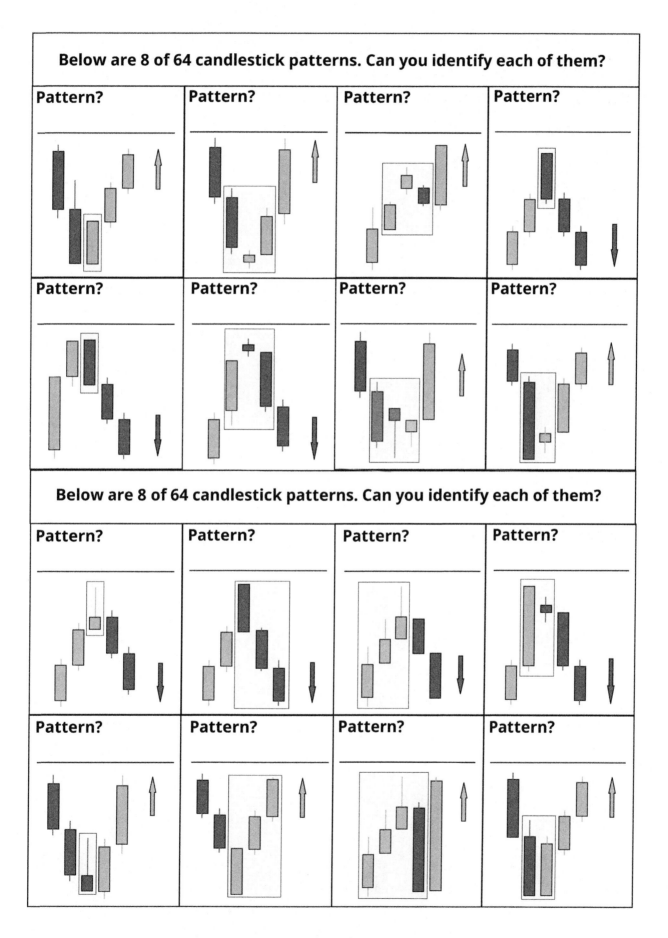

Below are 8 of 64 candlestick patterns. Can you identify each of them?

Pattern?	Pattern?	Pattern?	Pattern?

Pattern?	Pattern?	Pattern?	Pattern?

Below are 8 of 64 candlestick patterns. Can you identify each of them?

Pattern?	Pattern?	Pattern?	Pattern?

Pattern?	Pattern?	Pattern?	Pattern?

Below are 8 of 64 candlestick patterns. Can you identify each of them?

Pattern?	Pattern?	Pattern?	Pattern?
____	____	____	____

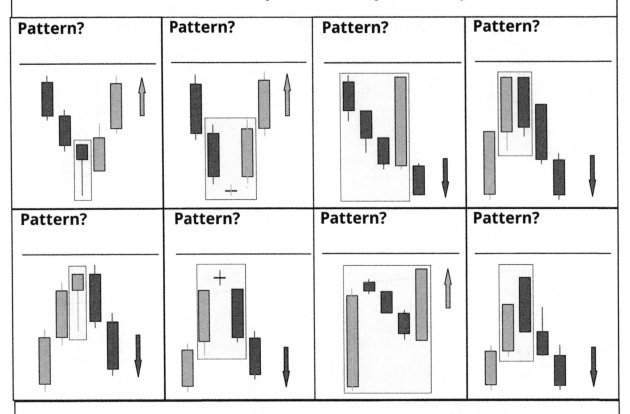

Below are 8 of 64 candlestick patterns. Can you identify each of them?

Pattern?	Pattern?	Pattern?	Pattern?
____	____	____	____

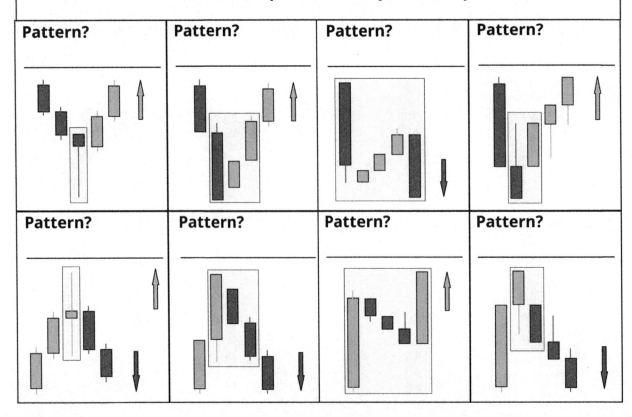

Below are 8 of 64 candlestick patterns. Can you identify each of them?

Pattern?	Pattern?	Pattern?	Pattern?
Pattern?	Pattern?	Pattern?	Pattern?

Below are 8 of 64 candlestick patterns. Can you identify each of them?

Pattern?	Pattern?	Pattern?	Pattern?
Pattern?	Pattern?	Pattern?	Pattern?

Below are 8 of 64 candlestick patterns. Can you identify each of them?

Pattern?	Pattern?	Pattern?	Pattern?

Pattern?	Pattern?	Pattern?	Pattern?

Below are 8 of 64 candlestick patterns. Can you identify each of them?

Pattern?	Pattern?	Pattern?	Pattern?

Pattern?	Pattern?	Pattern?	Pattern?

Did You Name Them All?

Chapter 9

Answers for Professional Challenge

Answers to Professional Challenge

Once you've completed the four challenges including this professional challenge and repeated until you are a 100% familiar with these common candlestick patterns, you will be more prepared to succeed as a day trader.

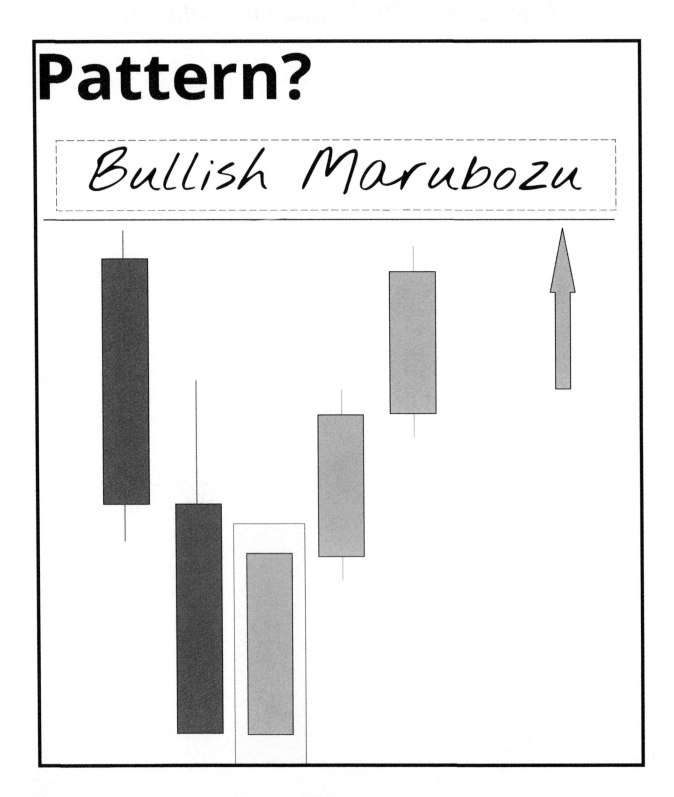

Pattern?

Bullish Marubozu

Answer to Challenge from Page 151

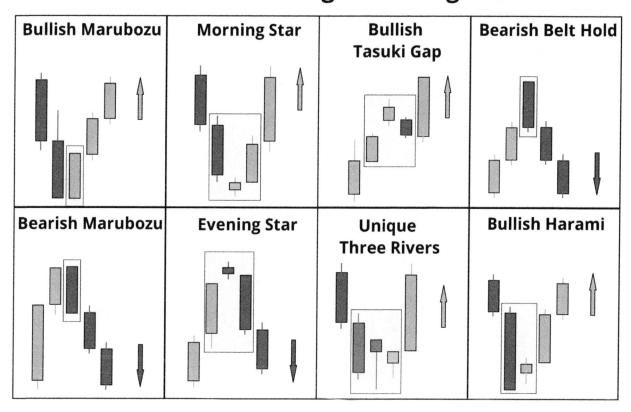

Bullish Marubozu	Morning Star	Bullish Tasuki Gap	Bearish Belt Hold
Bearish Marubozu	Evening Star	Unique Three Rivers	Bullish Harami

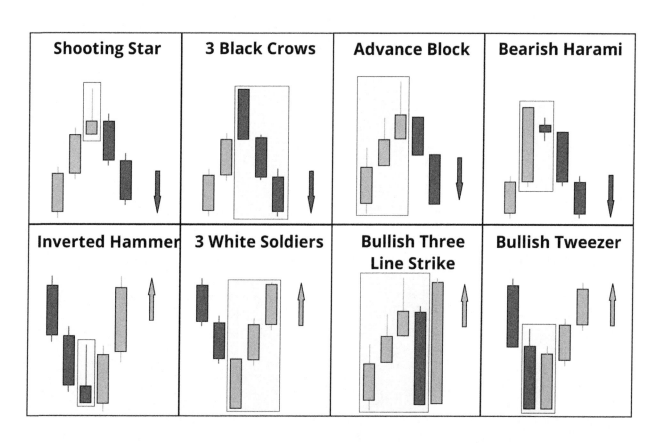

Shooting Star	3 Black Crows	Advance Block	Bearish Harami
Inverted Hammer	3 White Soldiers	Bullish Three Line Strike	Bullish Tweezer

Answer to Challenge from Page 152

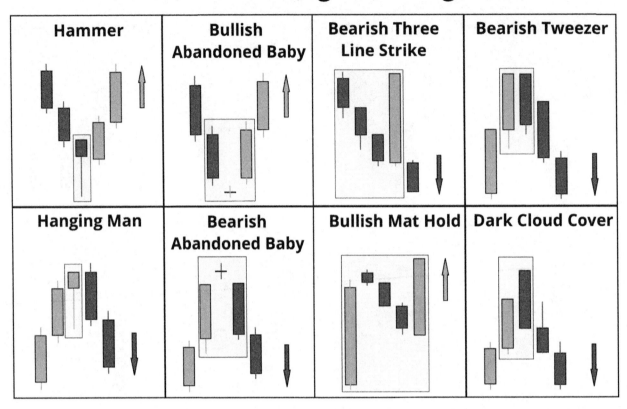

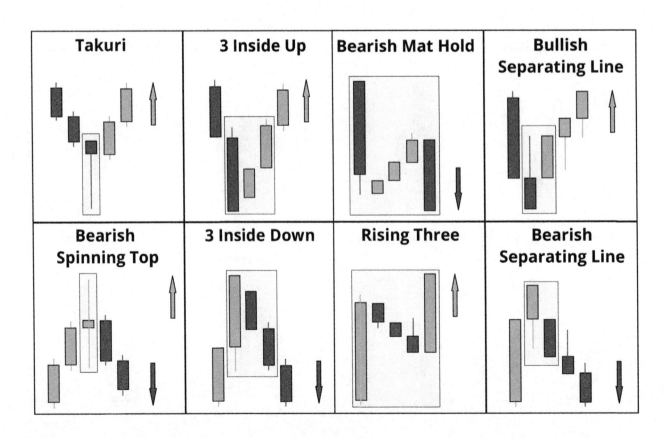

Answer to Challenge from Page 153

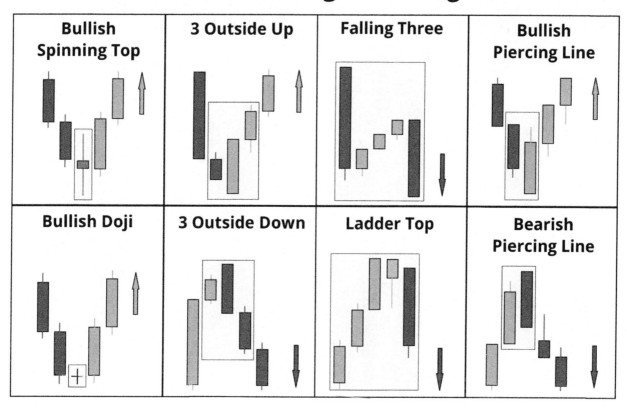

Bullish Spinning Top	3 Outside Up	Falling Three	Bullish Piercing Line
Bullish Doji	3 Outside Down	Ladder Top	Bearish Piercing Line

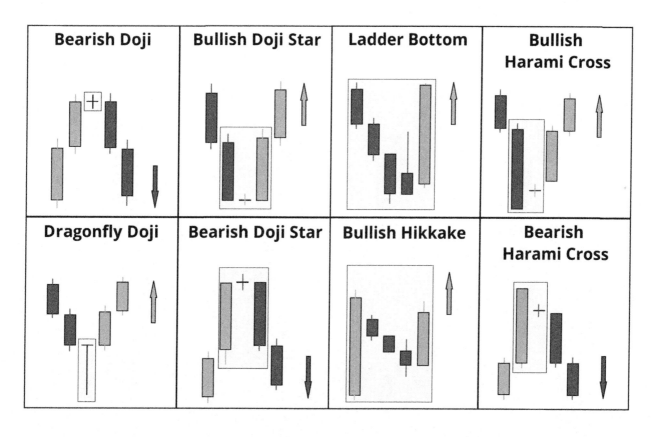

Bearish Doji	Bullish Doji Star	Ladder Bottom	Bullish Harami Cross
Dragonfly Doji	Bearish Doji Star	Bullish Hikkake	Bearish Harami Cross

Answer to Challenge from Page 154

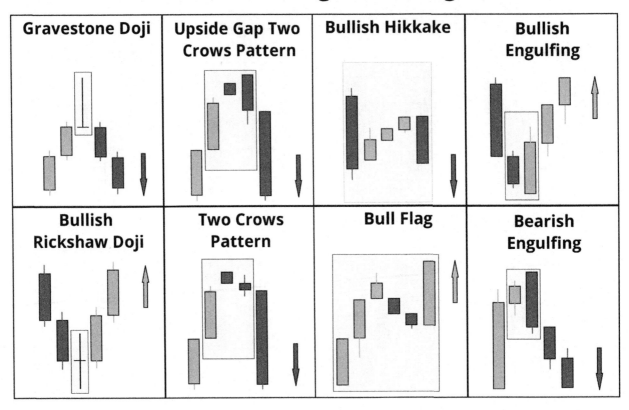

Gravestone Doji	Upside Gap Two Crows Pattern	Bullish Hikkake	Bullish Engulfing
Bullish Rickshaw Doji	**Two Crows Pattern**	**Bull Flag**	**Bearish Engulfing**

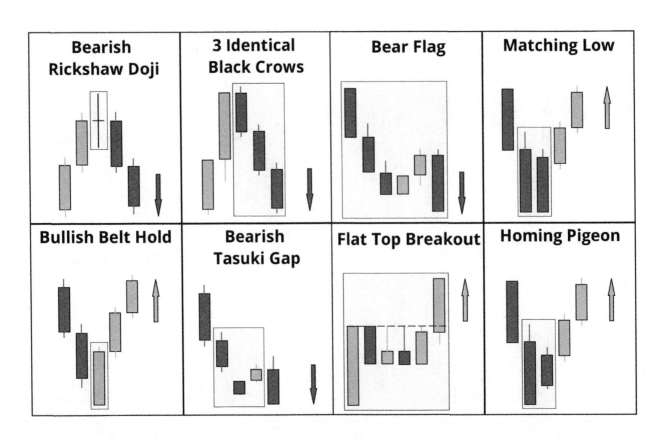

Bearish Rickshaw Doji	3 Identical Black Crows	Bear Flag	Matching Low
Bullish Belt Hold	**Bearish Tasuki Gap**	**Flat Top Breakout**	**Homing Pigeon**

Congratulations!

We would like to give special thanks to the individuals that helped with their creative ideas, editing insights and promotion of the Million-Dollar Margin Club books with their fantastic reviews

The Million-Dollar Margin Club is committed to releasing high quality, entertaining, and educational books. The MMC welcomes creative ideas and reviews from the trading community for their pre-published and even, already published books. Contributors' names can be immortalized in the pages of MMC publications.

If you would like to join the exclusive Million-Dollar Margin Club and participate in this unique opportunity,
please email:

mmcvisions@gmail.com
with the subject line
Join the MMC

If You Like the Book Don't Forget to Support the Author with a Great Review!

Thank You!

Glossary of Common Trading Terms

- **Average Directional Index (ADX)** – measures the strength of a trend, regardless of its direction, using price movements
- **Average True Range (ATR)** – measures volatility and range of price movement over a given period
- **Bar Chart** - represents price movements, where each bar (candle) denotes a specific time frame
- **Bear Market** – market condition where prices are falling or expected to fall
- **Bollinger Bands** – measures volatility and range relative to its moving average
- **Breakout** – When a security's price moves outside a predefined support or resistance level
- **Breakout Volume** – the volume of trades during a price breakout, confirms the breakout's strength
- **Bull Market** – market condition where prices are rising or expected to rise
- **Candlestick Chart** – displays the high, low, opening and closing price of a security for a specific period
- **Chart Patterns** – graphical formation created to identify price movement on a chart
- **Closing Price** – the final price a security is traded for in a given period or on a given day
- **Consolidation** – a period where prices move within a narrow range, indicating stability or indecision
- **Convergence and Divergence** – the movement of two or more indicators in relation to each other, used to predict future price movements
- **EMA** – Exponential Moving Average – tracks trend & support/resistance giving weight to more recent data
- **Fibonacci Retracements** – used to identify potential reversal levels on candlestick charts
- **Gap** – a break between prices on a chart when a security takes a sharp move up or down with no trading in between
- **Heikin-Ashi Technique** – modifies candles to reduce noise and clarify trend direction
- **High** – the highest price at which a security is traded during a specific period
- **Moving Average Convergence Divergence (MACD)** – a trend-following momentum indicator
- **Momentum Indicators** – track the speed of price changes in a security to identify trend strength
- **Open Price** – the starting price a security is traded for in a given period or on a given day
- **Oscillators** – indicators that vary within a band or range, typically identify overbought or oversold conditions
- **Pivot Points** – tracks support/resistance levels often showing a reversal of a current trend
- **Price Action** – movement of a security's price plotted over time
- **Relative Strength Index (RSI)** – tracks overbought/oversold conditions and momentum
- **Resistance Levels** – price level where selling pressure can overcome buying, halting rising prices
- **Stochastic Oscillator** – compares a security's closing price to its price range over a specific time measuring momentum
- **Support Levels** – a price level where buying pressure can overcome selling, halting falling prices
- **Symbol** – a unique identifier assigned to a security for trading purposes
- **Technical Analysis** – the study of past market data to forecast future price movements
- **Time Frame** – the duration for which a trading chart illustrates the price movements of a security
- **Trend** – the general direction in which a security's price is moving over a period of time
- **Trend Line** – a straight line that connects a series of price points and extends into the future to act as a line of support or resistance
- **Volume** – tracks the volume traded at different price levels within a specific time period
- **VWAP – Volume Weighted Average Price** – calculating a price over a specific time period and is commonly used by institutional investors and day traders to assess the value of an asset and make trading decisions

Printed in Great Britain
by Amazon

40415101R00099